THE
MODENA Ferrari ITALIA
automobili
HANDBOOK

compiled by

Hans Tanner

Copyright 2023 www.VelocePress.com

Published and Copyrighted 1960

FLOYD CLYMER PUBLICATIONS

1268 South Alvarado Street
Los Angeles 6, California

World's largest publisher of books pertaining to automobiles, motorcycles, motor racing and Americana.

Announcement

One of the outstanding and few remaining rugged individualists in the automotive field, especially in the competition field, is Enzo Ferrari of Modena, Italy.

Through the years the name of FERRARI has stood for quality merchandise and automobiles of unique design and construction that enjoy an enviable position the world over.

I have known Mr. Ferrari for many years, and some ten years ago visited his factory at Marinello, some 14 miles from his offices and showroom in the larger and better known city of Modena. I have been through almost every important automobile factory in the world and I could not help but admire the precision workmanship and the intense effort put into the production of Ferrari cars. Once could almost eat a meal off the spotlessly clean floor. The workmen, dressed in blue uniforms, might well be precision workmen in a fine watch or clock factory. Every tool seemed to be in its proper place, and thus the skilled workmen were able to find them instantly and with no lost motion or effort.

As automobile factories go, Ferrari is not a large one, but it is undoubtedly the finest specialized factory that I have ever visited.

Mr. Ferrari, a former competition driver and a capable engineer of many years standing, can and does build the type of sports and racing cars that he thinks should be built. His success proves that he knows what he is doing and, fortunately, makes his own decisions and does about as he pleases. He is a forceful and opinionated man who sleeps until noon and works half the night at his favorite hobby, and a hobby which has turned into a world-renowned and profitable business.

The author of this book, Hans Tanner, living in Modena, Italy, has access to the latest information on Italian and other European cars and he has done a fine job in compiling this Handbook.

I trust the reader finds it as interesting to read as I did in publishing it.

Floyd Clymer

*To
Gerard "Jabby" Crombac
Paris*

ACKNOWLEDGMENTS

I would like to thank the Scuderia Ferrari, Luigi Chinetti and Richie Ginther of Ferrari of California for their cooperaton in contributing material for this book. My thanks also to Bernard Cahier, Corrado Millanta, Jesse Alexander, Nino Barbieri, and Fototechnica for the photos provided.

Hans Tanner.

Introduction

The secret of keeping a Ferrari in good running order is to keep your "gold plated" screwdrivers out of the works.

Luigi Chinetti.

Enzo Ferrari at the wheel of the Alfa Romeo that he drove in the 1924 Coppa Acerbo race at Pescara, Italy

Enzo Ferrari, "The Master," as he looks today — 1959

PREFACE

The Ferrari Handbook is a compilation of specifications and statistical data as well as factory drawings assembled from various sources over a period of years by several ardent Ferrari enthusiasts. Though it is in no manner an attempt to encompass every model of Ferrari built, it is, however, an attempt to present a cross-section of the best, and most famous Ferraris built since 1948.

The specifications are presented in chronological order.

The reader will find herein specifications, action photos, sales promotion photos, candid pit-side photos, driving experiences, maintenance data, repair data, timing charts, lubrication charts, wiring diagrams, and cut-away drawings which will aid the owner, the enthusiast, and the occasional reader of sports car information.

TABLE OF CONTENTS

SECTION ONE — Driving Experiences 11

SECTION TWO — Specifications of Ferraris 1948 to 1958 19

SECTION THREE — Precautions and Adjustments 77

SECTION FOUR — Maintenance and tune-up suggestions 81

SECTION FIVE — Timing adjustments, various models .. 91

SECTION SIX — Acceleration times, various models 93

SECTION SEVEN — Detail drawings of major & minor components 106
   including electrical wiring and lubrication charts

Side view of the 250 G-T engine such as is used in the "California".

SECTION ONE
Driving Experiences with the Ferrari

THE TYPE 166

The first touring cars produced by Ferrari were the two-liter 12 cylinder type 166 cars. The basic 12 cylinder engine has been retained as a touring car engine for all Ferraris from the first model to date, and the engine displacement has been slowly increased from the original two-liter through 2.3, 2.5, 2.7, 3 lit, 4.1, 4.5, and 4.9 liter. This 12 cylinder engine was designed by Gioacchino Colombo, who had been associated with Ferrari in the latter's Alfa Romeo days and who had been on the design team responsible for the famous 158 x 1500cc supercharged Alfa Romeo Grand Prix car, the team comprised of Vittorio Jano (designer of the Lancia GP car) and Ing Massimino, formerly of Maserati and Alfa Romeo. Since designing the 12-cylinder Ferrari Colombo has been responsible for the six-cylinder two-liter GP Maserati, the Alfa Romeo Disco Volante, and the GP Bugatti.

My first experiences with Ferraris were with the Marzotto-owned two-liter type 166, from this I went on to the rather disappointing 2.3-liter which was the first Ferrari in England, owned by Roy Clarkson. The first drive in a 2.5-liter which became Ferrari's first "production car" was on a Swiss-owned, one-off, short-wheelbase model which had rather curious handling characteristics. However, when Mike Hawthorn joined the Ferrari team, and consequently purchased a 2.5-liter for his own transportation we completed over 3000 miles of road driving together, most of this being in practice for the 1953 Mille Miglia, and many trips over the Futa Pass from Bologne to Florence. This car was a type 212 Inter with a "superleggera" body by Touring of Milan, having been built in the period before Ferrari used Ghia and Vignale bodies on his cars. The instrument panel had two large dials on either side, one on the left showing the RPM from 0-8500, and the one on the right kilometers per hour from 0-240. Contained within these are small gages showing water temperature, oil pressure, fuel content, and a small clock. An added fitting on Mike's car was an "average speed meter," however these instruments had an annoying habit of going wrong after a week, and from then on never seemed to function at all.

Despite the car's racing parentage, starting presents none of the problems usually associated with racing cars. A quick stab at the starter button, and the engine responds with a muffled growl, the screaming being eliminated by the very efficient Abarth mufflers. Light pressure on the single plate clutch allows first gear to be engaged, and great care must be taken with the accelerator otherwise the take off is accompanied by a certain amount of wheelspin. It is even possible to spin the wheels in fifth gear on this car. The gearbox is somewhat of a problem until the driver has had a certain amount of practice with it, and although third and fourth gears are synchromesh, selection can be accompanied by anything except the silence claimed for it. Hawthorn naturally mastered these peculiarities rapidly, and adopted a system of flicking the gears with his fingers, having an especially rapid action for the very tricky fifth-to-fourth shift.

Good acceleration through the gears, and extreme docility of this model make it a good traffic car. Speed in fifth gear can be dropped to about ten mph from which the consequent acceleration evokes no protest from the engine. The suspension however is rather hard for those used to a modern car, being the same on the Ferrari as on the sports cars.

During our first lap of practice for the Mille Miglia we cruised all day long over the straight roads from Brescia to Pescara between 85 and 95 mph. On our second run however despite a return trip to the factory to fix a broken head gasket, we were frequently at 110 and on several of the really long and clear stretches we had the car to 120 mph. In the mountains between Aquila and Rome we had considerable amount of trouble passing another competitor practicing in a Lancia Gran Turismo, whose roadholding was considerably better than ours on the tight uphill curves.

The engine was responsible for a great deal of noise, most of it coming from the camshaft drive. The Pirelli racing tires, too, added to the noise in general, however it was possible to talk in the car. I had ample experience of the comforts of riding in the so-called back seat of the car, when we picked up the late Tom Cole at Milan airport and drove him to Modena some 125 miles away. I did, however, recover from the experience after a few weeks, but still bear a permanent mark on my head from the pneumatic drill action of my skull against the "beautiful lines" of the roof, despite being bent double. No complaints about this car really be made, for although Ferrari has built some full four-seaters, these are few and far between, and he has openly stated his dislike for cars of this type. Although the 2.5-liter type Inter had its vices and defects, it was certainly the one Ferrari from which I had the most enjoyment.

TYPES 342 AND 340 AMERICA

After the initial successes of his type 166 Mille Miglia and Inter two-liter cars, Ferrari turned his eye to the American market. However his first efforts in the USA did not meet with all the success expected. Chief stumbling block in competition motoring was the Allard with its variety of engines up to the five-liter Cadillac porving more than a match for the smaller capacity Ferraris on the American type circuits. Ferrari then turned to what seemed the obvious answer to the problem, increasing the cubic inch displacement of his cars. For this purpose he built a larger engine employing all 'round larger basic castings and parts, the car called the 342 America.

The car in its first appearances was not particularly successful and lacked speed, but by subsequent development the bad points in the design were rectified and the car renamed the 340 America became a real performer and soon sounded the death knell of its British competitor, the Allard.

The 342 America had the classic V12, 60 degree engine, with a bore and stroke of 80 x 68mm. It had a total displacement of 4101.66cc, and with a compression ratio of 8:1, gave a total of 200BHP at 5000 RPM. The chassis frame, constructed by the firm of Colombo in Milan, was of monobloc construction and comprised a steel elliptic section tubular structure.

Open sports bodies were built for this car by Touring of Milan who had been responsible for both coupes and sports bodies on the type 166 Mille Miglia and Inter models, and the 4.1 Sports could only be distinguished from its two-liter brother by its overall size. Bodies for the touring cars were built first by Ghia and then later by Vignale. The Ghia-bodied cars were the nearest thing to full 4 seaters that Ferrari ever built.

In the meantime Ferrari had been developing the 4.1-liter to give much more power and a general better performance, the 342 America with the 12/42 rear axle and 6.40 x 15 tires gave a maximum speed of 115 mph at 5000 RPM in fourth gear which was not very impressive for such a large capacity car.

The original bore stroke of 80 x 68mm was retained, as was the compression ratio of 8:1, but the RPM range was increased from 5000 RPM to 6500 RPM the result being an increase of 60 BHP bringing the figure to 260 BHP. A five-speed gearbox was fitted with the following ratios: 1st 12.3; 2nd 7.60; 3rd 5.52; 4th 4.00; 5th 3.70. A double dry plate clutch replaced the original single plate variety, and the net result was a car capable of 150 mph, and quite capable of taking on the Allards. Naturally, development did not cease at this point, and experiments continued in the racing versions through the fabulous 340 Mexico and 340 Mille Miglia cars.

Of these cars I had the opportunity of testing a type 342 America with a Ghia body, and a type 340 America with Vignale body. The first car was the one belonging to Sir James Scott Douglas, who had acquired the car from David Brown, builder of Aston Martins. The car was a four-seater version and had been used by David Brown for experimental purposes in connection with Aston Martin and Lagonda construction. The second car was the two-seater Vignale coupe belonging to Vincent of Paris, which I was able to test while the car was in the possession of French racing driver Renee Marchand. The Scott-Douglas car was finished in dark blue and silver, whereas the Vincent car was painted in French racing blue.

I collected the Scott-Douglas car from Cannes, for the purpose of driving it to Milan to replace the dynamo drive bushings, and then deliver it to the owner in Paris. From the first moment I had constant trouble with the car, and chronic misfiring was only rectified by a complete change of plugs, which process involved several burnt fingers on the hot engine. The car heated badly while crossing the mountains between Menton and Turin and several stops had to be made to cool it off. Driving was rather uncomfortable due to the bench-type front seat which caused me to slide sideways when the car went around a corner. While cornering at high speed the car also has a tendency to lift its offside rear wheel, however the defects revealed in tight cornering were made up by the car's steady performance on the straight Turin Milan Autostrada where good acceleration took the car quickly to its maximum 5000 RPM in fourth gear to a speed of approximately 115 mph, at which pace the car would cruise happily all day. I experienced a certain amount of trouble with the shock absorbers which made the front end behavior somewhat rough, and which caused the car's body to bang continuously against the chassis.

Most of thse defects were rectified in the type 340 America except that the lighter and less luxurious Vignale body transmitted very much more noise, and questionable body construction also contributed more than its own share of squeaks and groans. The car with its increased power and five-speed gearbox was considerably more lively, and bucket seats were a great aid to driving. Acceleration was very quick and crisp, although not as impressive as that of the three-liter type 250. At Montlhery near Paris I completed several laps at just under 130 mph, the car giving a very uncomfortable ride, and being rather frightening on the very pronounced bumps on the top part of the banking. Had a better surface been available I am certain that very close to the 150 mph could have been reached with this car.

The first series Ferrari 250 Europa was based on the 4.1-liter 340 America engine with the block and cylinder head suitably modified. Late in 1954 when Mercedes, with the 300SL, were developing their challenge in the Gran Turismo class, Ferrari decided to go into production with 100 examples of a three-liter touring car, the 250 Europa series two. In the second series, however, the type 250 Mille Miglia engine was used as a basis. This engine is a direct descendant from all the earlier 12-cylinder engines, in fact the stroke of 58.8mm which had been introduced with the earliest two-liter type 166 Mille Miglia, and carried on with the 195 Inter, 212 Export, and 212 Inter was retained. Apart from being lighter, it was considerably more powerful than series one, and was of proved reliability. Modifications were made to reduce engine noise to meet touring requirements, and other modifications included detail chassis alterations and the fitting of a fully synchromesh gearbox, and general internal refinements. The three-liter "small" engine is in the classic Ferrari sixty degree V12 style, with a bore and stroke of 73mm by 58.8mm giving a total displacement of 2953.21cc. The compression ratio is 8.5 to 1 and the power output of these models was raised to 240 bhp at 7200 rpm.

I was able to test three examples. The first was the prototype with which Luigi Chinetti and I completed over 1300 miles from Florida to New York. The second car I tested at Modena in town, and on the Autodrome with Sergio Sighinolfi, the Ferrari works chief tester. The car was one of the full production types out for its final test a few hours before delivery to the customer. The third was the Marquis de Portagos' specially prepared car which was entered for the production car race at Nassau.

Chinetti's car had been shipped to Sebring, Florida, for racing. It was the same handsome design that was adopted with slight variations for the complete series of 100 cars, finished in dove grey with grey cloth interior. This particular car had not been equipped with the fully synchromesh box but had wire wheels with polished aluminum rims and chromed hubs and spokes. Chinetti and I set off in the evening driving at a steady 65 mph. Two things struck me immediately about this prototype, the quietness of the engine and the frightful tire noise caused by the racing Engleberts fitted for Sebring. Another noticeable thing was the whine from the gearbox which on occasion sounded like a turbojet taking off. This noise was completely eliminated, however, in the synchro box on the production type I tried later. The car was strikingly comfortable and it lacked that hard bouncing ride so often experienced in the earlier types of touring Ferraris.

The continuous variation of speed laws in the different states, varying from 70 mph to 55 mph, made the run more like a test for handling at touring speeds, for town driving and for the location of various noises. There was the odd opportunity for opening up, and several times we reached 130-135 mph without using the full rpm in fourth gear. This should indicate that the car is capable of approximately 140 mph. At these speeds, however, the voice of the engine was considerably more pronounced, and even with the very large exhaust mufflers there was a certain amount of booming. The gasoline consumption for the whole trip averaged out at 15½ miles per gallon.

The test on the second car was carried out in Modena. Sighinolfi drove the car through the multitude of narrow Modenese back streets and completed several laps of the Modena Autodrome. The car was fitted with a full synchromesh gearbox, and was finished in dark red and cream with chromed wire wheels. The interior was superbly finished in leather, complete with heater and de-mister ducts. The new type Nardi steering wheel, which is now standard, is a beautiful example of craftsmanship and replaces the earlier type wheel which was the same on the Grand Prix cars.

Sighinolfi first drove me around the outskirts of Modena at various speeds, mainly to show the complete flexibility of the engine in fourth gear, slowing down almost to a standstill and accelerating away smoothly and rapidly under all conditions. When driving through the narrow cobblestoned streets of Modena, involving frequent stopping and starting, there was absolutely no sign of overheating, and the electric fan was not used. In an incredibly short time the speed would be back to 60 mph or more.

We then proceded to the Autodrome where Sighinolfi holds the unofficial lap record on the Grand Prix "Supersqualo" Ferrari. On the first lap he took things fairly quietly, taking the opportunity of clearing the track of two peasants who were walking down the middle of it, carrying loads of hay about ten times their size. On the second lap, coming into the pits straight, he really got to work.

At the braking point for the chicane 105 mph was indicated. He took the double bend as he would with the Grand Prix car, and the touring car behaved perfectly (accompanied by a very strong smell of burnt rubber), then through the long curve he put the car into a drift. On reaching the main straight, 122 mph was indicated. Speed went up to 134 mph before it was necessary to brake for the left-hand corner, which was taken with equal verve. The car gave a wonderful feeling of stability. Even when driven like a Grand Prix car, there was no inclination to grab frantically to hold on to something and to avoid going out of the door—or ending up in the driver's lap. Going up the pit straight, we accelerated to over 100 mph. Sighinolfi took his hands off the steering wheel, and folded his arms. The car continued on a straight line with absolutely no reaction at all from the road wheels. During the test the only noticeable noise was the exhaust note, the gearbox whine had been completely eliminated and the tire noise was negligible on this car. It would be difficult to find another car with a sports/racing performance such as this has, and yet it is so flexible and docile for touring purposes, a quality somewhat lacking in several of the other touring models of Ferrari.

TYPE 375 AMERICA

At the same time that Ferrari produced his finalized version of the 4.1-liter type 340 Mille Miglia, he was already experimenting with a 4.5-liter version. This car made its appearance at Senigallia in 1953 with an open Vignale body very similar to the customers' version of the 340 Mille Miglia, with which Marzotto won that year's Mille Miglia. The factory cars had open bodies by Touring of Milan. The car was very impressive, Villoresi driving it had a lead of 11 seconds on the first lap from Marzotto and Ruesch on the 4.1 liter Mille Miglia cars. Transmission trouble put the car out, but at Pescara the first coupe version appeared with a body by Pinin Farina (the car driven by Hawthorn and Maglioli), led the 12-hour race from start to finish. Ferrari then decided to go into limited construction of touring versions of these cars which were to be called 375 Americas as opposed to the 375 Mille Miglia which was the racing brother of the car.

The engine was the classic Ferrari V-12 60-degree, with a bore and stroke of 84 x 68mm, the displacement was 4498cc, and with a compression ratio of 8:1 it gave 300 BHP at 6300 rpm. Bodies for these cars were built either by Vignale, or Pinin Farina. All the bodies of this series of cars were very distinctive—the strangest being the one built by Farina for Roberto Rossellini, the Italian film producer. One of these 4.5-liter type 375 Americas was purchased by John Shakespeare. The car had a good looking body, finished in yellow and fawn by Vignale.

I had several drives in John Shakespeare's car, and noticed immediately the great improvement over the types 342 and 340 America. Vignale had taken much more care in the building of the luxurious body, but nevertheless the car was not as perfect as the later three-liter 250 Europa cars built by Farina. Despite careful checking there were still some squeaks and rattles present in the body, the chief offender being the steering column which rattled in its metal sheath. Performance-wise the car was a vast improvement over the earlier models, the acceleration from very low speeds was really phenomenal and with the very efficient Grand Prix brakes the car could be slowed as easily as it could be accelerated. The limited-slip differential made all the difference in power transmission and the car was much more stable at high speed both on the straight, and on rapid cornering. The car would cruise along happily on the parkway at 2000 rpm and could be brought down to about 15 mph in fourth gear and lose none of its snappy getaway. Gear-shifting was also a happier experience and no great skill was needed. High speed test runs resulted in 155 mph being reached on several occasions without full throttle being used, this would indicate that the factory-advertised maximum speed of 165 mph might be easily attainable.

The 375 America Touring car with its tremendous performance gave me the overall impression of being much more like a full-blooded competition car than any other touring Ferrari built to that date.

SECTION TWO
Ferrari Specifications   —1948 to 1958

TYPE 125 SPORTS (1948)

Engine V 12 cylinder, 60 deg, bore & stroke 55 x 52mm. Displacement 1498cc; Compression ratio 9:1; Max BHP 118; Max RPM 6500; cranckase aluminum light alloy, with pressed-in cast iron liners, cylinder head light alloy with hemispherical combustion chambers, crankshaft high resistance steel, counterbalanced supported on 7 bearings one of which is designed for axial support. Timing, inclined overhead valves actuated through rocker arms from a single overhead camshaft for each bank of cylinders. Camshafts driven by silent chain with semi-automatic tensioning. Lubrication forced by gear type pump, thermostatically controlled oil radiator, filter, and permanently adjusted pressure-limiting valve. One Weber twin-choke type 32 DCF carburetor, electric starting with starting button on dashboard, single plug per cylinder, 2 Marelli distributors. AC mechanical fuel pump, engine supported on four rubber mounts.

Clutch Single dry-plate type.

Gearbox in unit with engine, 5 forward speers and reverse. Countershaft gear 22/29. Gear ratios 1st 2.41, 2nd 1.74, 3rd 1.27, 4th 1.00, 5th 0.925, rev 3.1. Oil pump and filter incorported in gearbox.

Transmission two piece with central support.

Rear Axle Rigid type with central light alloy casing containing the differential assembly.

Steering With parallel motion independent of wheel oscillation, worm screw and helical gear.

Front Suspension Independent, with double wishbones and single transverse leaf spring. Damping by low pressure hydraulic shock absorbers.

Rear Suspension Semi-elliptic leaf springs, low pressure hydraulic shock absorbers.

Brakes pedal operated, hydraulic on all 4 wheels, single master cylinder, single pump drum type, hand operated mechanical on rear wheels.

Frame Monobloc, steel circular section tubular structure. Wheelbase 95.2 ins; tread, front 48.2 ins., rear 47.2 ins.; tires front 5.00 x 15; rear 5.50 x 15.

The 1948 Type 166 "Sports" Ferarri Race Car

The 1948 Type 166 Ferrari Roadster

TYPE 166 SPORTS (1948)

Engine V 12 cylinder, 60 degree Bore, Stroke 60 x 58.8 mm. Displacement 1995 cc, compression ratio 10:1. Max BHP 140. Max RPM 6600. Crankcase aluminum light alloy, with pressed-in cast iron liners. Cylinder head light alloy with hemispherical combustion chambers. Crankshaft high resistance steel, counterbalanced, supported on 7 bearings one of which is designed for axial support. Timing, inclined overhead valves actuated through rocker arms from a single overhead camshaft for each bank of cylinders. Camshafts driven by a silent chain with semi automatic tensioning. Lubrication is forced by gear type pump, thermostatically controlled oil radiator, filter, and permanently adjusted pressure limiting valve. Three Weber twin choke type 36 DCF carburetors, electric starting with starter button on dashboard, single plug per cylinder. 2 Marelli magnetos. AC mechanical type fuel pump. Engine supported on four rubber mounts.

Clutch Single dry plate with elastic hub.

Gearbox in unit with engine, 5 forward speeds and reverse. Countershaft gear 22/29. Gear ratios 1st 2.41, 2nd 1.74, 3rd 1.27, 4th 1.00, 5th 0.925, rev 3.1. Oil pump and filter incorporated in gearbox.

Transmission shaft Two piece with central support and three universals.

Rear Axle Fixed type with central light alloy casing containing the differential assembly.

Steering with parallel motion independent of wheel oscillation, worm screw and helical gear.

Front Suspension Independent, with double wishbones and single transverse leaf spring. Damping by low pressure hydraulic shock absorbers.

Rear Suspension Semi elliptic leaf springs, low pressure hydraulic shock absorbers and torsional stabilizing bar.

Brakes pedal-operated, hydraulic on 4 wheels, single master cylinder, single pump drum type, hand operated mechanical on rear drums for parking.

Frame Monobloc steel elliptic section tubular structure. Wheelbase 88.5 ins.; tread, front 50, rear 49.2 ins., dry weight 1780 lbs.; tires 5:50 x 15 front & rear; right-hand drive; fuel capacity 20 gals.

The 1948 Type 166 "Millemiglia" Berlinetta by Vignale

The 1949 Type 1500 Formula 1 Grand Prix Race Car

*Ascari's Formula 1 1949 1500 Grand Prix engine
with two-stage blower*

TYPE 1500 F-1 (Formula 1 Grand Prix) 1949

V 12 cylinder 60 degree. Bore stroke 55 x 52.5 mm, displacement 1498 cc. Compression ratio 6.5:1. Max BHP 300. Max RPM 7500. Crankcase aluminum light alloy. Cylinder head light alloy with hemispheric combustion chamber. Crankshaft on 7 bearings one of which is for axial support. Inclined overhead valves actuated by twin overhead camshafts per bank. Camshafts gear driven. Hairpin valve springs. Two Rootes type blowers mounted one above the other in front of the engine, the top one feeding the intake pipe situated between the blocks. Single plug per cylinder centrally disposed and supplied by two horizontal magnetos driven from the rear of the engine. 5 speed and reverse gearbox in unit with engine. Front suspension is by double wishbones with single transverse leaf spring mounted below and coupled to top wishbone by a tubular link. Swing axles at rear with transverse leaf spring mounted above axle. Integral Houdaille shock absorbers. Single radius arms locate axle. Chassis frame oval section tubular. Two leading shoe drum brakes. Wheelbase 85 ins.; tread, front 50, rear 49.2 ins.

The 1949 Type 166 "Formula Libre" Sports Coupe by Vignale

TYPE 166 F-LIBRE (Formula Libre) (1949)

Engine V 12 cylinder, 60 degree. Bore, stroke 60 x 58.8 mm. Displacement 1995 cc. Compression ration 7.5:1. Max BHP 110. Max RPM 6000. Crankcase aluminum light alloy, with pressed-in cast iron liners. Cylinder head light alloy with hemispherical combustion chambers. Crankshaft high resistance steel, counterbalanced, supported on 7 bearings one of which designed for axial support. Timing, inclined overhead valves actuated through rocker arms from a single overhead camshaft per bank of cylinders. Camshafts driven by silent chain with semi-automatic tensioning. Lubrication forced by gear type pump, thermostatically controlled oil radiator, filter, and permanently adjusted pressure-limiting valve. One twin choke type 32 DCF Weber carburetor. Electric starting, with starter button on dashboard. Single plug per cylinder. 2 distributors and two HT coils. AC type R/101 mechanical fuel pump. Engine supported on 4 rubber mounts.

Clutch Single dry plate type with elastic hub.

Gearbox in unit with engine. 5 forward speeds and reverse. 3rd and 4th gears synchronized. Countershaft gear 19/32. Gear Ratios 1st 3.08, 2nd 1.9, 3rd 1.38, 4th 1.00, 5th 0.925, rev 3.1. Oil pump and filter incorporated in gearbox.

Transmission shaft Two piece with central support and three universals.

Rear axle fixed type with central light alloy casing containing the differential assembly.

Steering with parallel motion independent of wheel oscillation, worm screw and helical gear.

Front Suspension Independent, with double wishbones and single transverse leaf spring. Damping by low pressure hydraulic shock absorbers.

Rear suspension Semi elliptic leaf springs, low pressure hydraulic shock absorbers and torsional stabilizing bar.

Brakes pedal operated, hydraulic on 4 wheels, single master cylinder, single pump drum type, hand operated mechanical on the rear drums for parking.

Frame Monobloc steel elliptic section tubular structure. Wheelbase 85 ins. Tread, front 50, rear 49.2 ins.; tires 5:50 x 16 front, 7:00 x 16 rear. Dry weight 1630 lbs.; fuel capacity 44 gals.

TYPE 195 SPORTS (1949)

Engine V 12 cylinder, 60 degree; Bore, Stroke 65 x 58.8 mm. Displacement 2340 cc. Compression ration 7.5:1. Max BHP 130. Max RPM 6000. Crankcase aluminum light alloy, with pressed-in cast iron liners. Cylinder head light alloy with hemispherical combustion chambers. Crankshaft high resistance steel, counterbalanced, supported on 7 bearings, one of which is designed for axial support. Timing, inclined overhead valves actuated through rocker arms from a single overhead camshaft for each bank of cylinders. Camshafts driven by silent chain with semi-automatic tensioning. Lubrication forced by gear type pump, thermostatically controlled oil radiator, filter, and permanently adjusted pressure limiting valve. One twin choke type 32 DCF Weber carburetor. Electric starting, with starter button on dashboard. Single plug per cylinder, 2 distributors and 2 HT coils. AC type R/101 mechanical fuel pump. Engine supported on 4 rubber mounts.

Clutch Single dry plate type with elastic hub.

Gearbox in unit with engine. 5 forward speeds and reverse, 3rd and 4th synchronized. Countershaft gear 19/32. Gear ratios, 1st 3.08, 2nd 1.9, 3rd 1.38, 4th 1.00, 5th 0.925, rev 3.1. Oil pump and filter incorporated in gearbox.

Transmission shaft Two piece with central support and three universals.

Rear axle fixed type with central light alloy casing containing the differential assembly.

Chassis of the 1949 Type 195 "Inter" V-12

Steering with parallel motion independent of wheel oscillation, worm screw and helical gear.

Front Suspension Independent, with double wishbones and single transverse leaf spring. Damping by low pressure hydraulic shock absorbers.

Rear Suspension Semi-elliptic longitudinal springs, low pressure hydraulic shock absorbers and torional stabilizing bar.

Brakes pedal operated, hydraulic on 4 wheels, single master cylinder. Single pump drum type. Hand operated mechanical on the rear drums for parking.

Frame Monobloc steel elliptic section tubular structure. Wheelbase: 98.4 ins.; tread, front 50, rear 49.2 ins.; tries front & rear 5:90 x 15. Dry weight 2090 lbs.; fuel capacity 23 gals.

The 1949 Type 212 Ferrari "Sports" Coupe

TYPE 212 SPORTS (1949)
(Manufactured in 1950 as SPORTS, in 1952 and 1953 as EXPORT model)

Engine V 12 cylinder, 60 degree. Bore Stroke 68 x 58.8. Displacement 2562.51 cc. Compression ratio 8:1. Max BHP 150. Max RPM 6500. Crankcase aluminum light alloy with pressed-in cast iron liners. Cylinder head light alloy with hemispherical combustion chambers, crankshaft high resistance steel, counterbalanced, supported on 7 bearings, one of which designed for axial support. Timing, inclined overhead valves actuated through rocker arms from a single overhead camshaft for each bank of cylinders. Camshafts driven by silent semi-automatically tensioned chain. Lubrication forced by gear type pump, thermostatically controlled oil radiator, filter, and permanently adjusted pressure limiting valve. One Weber twin choke type 36 DCF carburetor. Electric starting with ignition key and starter button on dashboard. Single plug per cylinder. 2 distributors and 2 HT coils. FISPA type membrane mechanical fuel pump. Engine supported on 4 antivibration silent blocs.

Clutch single dry plate type with elastic hub.

Gearbox in unit with engine. 5 forward speeds and reverse. Countershaft gear 31/18. Gear ratios 1st 3.157, 2nd 1.946, 3rd 1.403, 4th 1.00, 5th 0.914, rev 4.058. Oil pump and filter incorporated in gearbox.

Transmission Shaft Two piece centrally supported, incorporates elastic torsional joint.

Rear Axle Fixed type with central light alloy casting containing the differential assembly.

Steering with parallel motion independent of wheel oscillation, worm screw drive and helical gear.

Front Suspension Independent with wishbones and single transverse leaf springs, integral rubber blocks, and damping by Houdaille shock absorbers.

Rear Suspension Semi elliptic longitudinal leaf springs, damping by Houdaille shock absorbers.

Brakes pedal operated hydraulic on 4 wheels. One master cylinder, single brake pump drum type. Hand-operated mechanical on rear wheels for parking.

Frame Monobloc steel elliptic section tubular structure. Wheelbase 88.5 ins.; tread, front 50, rear 49.2 ins.; tires 5:90 x 15 front & rear; dry weight 1760 lbs., fuel capacity 33 gals.

TYPE 275 SPORTS (1949) 3.3 Litre

V 12 cylinder 60 degrees. Bore Stroke 72 x 68 mm. Displacement 3300cc. Compression ratio 11:1. Max BHP 260. Max RPM 6500. Crankcase Aluminum light alloy. Cylinder head light alloy with screwed-in liners and hemispherical combustion chambers. Crankshaft on 7 bearings one of which is for axial support. Inclined overhead valves actuated through rocker arms by single overhead camshaft for each bank of cylinders. Camshafts chain driven, hairpin valve springs. Single plug per cylinder supplied by two Marelli magnetos, three Weber twin choke type 38DCF carburetors, 5 speed and reverse gearbox in unit with engine. Front suspension is by double wishbones with single transverse leaf spring mounted below and coupled to top wishbone by tubular link. Swing axles at rear with transverse leaf spring mounted above the axle. Integral Houdaille shock absorbers. Single radius arms locate the axle. Chassis frame oval section tubular structure. 2 leading shoe drum brakes. Wheelbase 94 ins.; tread 50½ ins.

TYPE 340 F-1 (Formula 1) (1950)
4.1 Litre Grande Prix, Unsupercharged

V 12 cylinder 60 degree, Bore, Stroke 80 x 68 mm; displacement 4080 cc, compression ratio 11:1, Max BHP 310, Max RPM 6500. Crankcase aluminum alloy. Cylinder head light alloy with hemispherical combustion chambers. Crankshaft 7 bearings, one of which is for axial support. Inclined overhead valves actuated through rocker arms by single overhead camshaft for each bank of cylinders. Camshafts chain driven. Hairpin valve springs. Single plug per cylinder supplied by two Marelli magnetos. Three Weber twin choke type 38 DCF carburetors. 4 speed and reverse gearbox in unit with ZF differential assembly. Front suspension is by double wishbones with a single transverse leaf spring mounted below and coupled to top wishbone by tubular link.

De Dion rear axle with transverse leaf spring mounted below, integral Houdaille shock absorbers. De Dion tube located by roller running in vertical guide on rear fame cross member and bronze pad in guide on differential casing. Parallel radius rods run forward to chassis frame from hub carriers. Chassis oval section tubular structure. 2 leading shoe drum brakes.

Wheelbase 90 ins. Front tread 50 ins, rear tread 48 ins.

Type 375 Formula 1 Grand Prix Race Car of 1950

TYPE 375 F-1 (Formula 1) (1950)
4.5 liter Grand Prix unsupercharged single ignition.

V 12 cylinder, 60 degree. Bore & Stroke 80 x 74.5 mm, displacement 4,498cc. Max BHP 330. Max RPM 7000. Crankcase aluminum light alloy. Cylinder head light alloy with screwed-in liners, hemispherical combustion chambers. Crankshaft on 7 ebarings one of which is for axial support. Inclined overhead valves actuated through rocker arms by single overhead camshaft for each bank of cylinders. Camshafts chain driven. Hairpin valve springs. Single plug per cylinder supplied by two Marelli magnetos. Three Weber twin-choke type carburetors. 4-speed and reverse gearbox in unit with ZF differential assembly. Front suspension is by double wishbones with single transverse leaf spring mounted below and coupled to top wishbone by tubular link.

De Dion rear axle with transverse leaf spring mounted below chassis, integral Houdaille shock absorbers. De Dion tube located by roller running in vertical guide on rear frame cross member and bronze pad in guide on differential casing. Parallel radius rods run forward to chassis frame from hub carriers. Chassis tubular rectangular section side members, circular section cross members.

Wheelbase 90 ins. Front tread 50 ins., rear tread 48 ins.

Type 375 Formula 1 Grand Prix Race Car of 1951

TYPE 375 F-1 (Formula 1) (1951)
4.5 liter Grand Prix, unsupercharged twin ignition

V 12 cylinder, 60 degree. Bore & stroke 80 x 74.5 mm; displacement 4,498 cc. Compression ratio 13:1. Max BHP 380; Max RPM 7000. Crankcase aluminum light alloy. Cylinder head light alloy with screwed-in liners, hemispherical combustion chambers. Crankshaft on 7 bearings one of which is for axial support. Inclined overhead valves actuated through rocker arms by single overhead camshaft for each bank of cylinders. Camshafts chain driven. Hairpin valve springs, two plugs per cylinder supplied by single aircraft type magneto driven from front end of engine. Three Weber type carburetors. Front suspension is by double wishbones with a single transverse leaf spring mounted below and coupled to top wishbone by tubular link. De Dion rear axle with transverse leaf spring mounted below chassis. Integral Houdaille shock absorbers. De Dion tube located by roller running in vertical guide on differential casing. Parallel radius rods run forward to chassis frame from hub carriers. Chassis frame tubular rectangular section side members. Circular section cross members. Two leading shoe drum type brakes. Wheelbase 90 ins. Front tread 50 ins., Rear tread 48 ins.

Type 166 Formula 2 Race Car of 1951

TYPE 166 F-2 (Formula 2) (1951)
2 liter unblown, De Dion rear axle.

V 12 cylinder 60 degree. Bore & stroke 63 x 52.5 mm; displacement 1995 cc. Compression ratio 11:1. Max BHP 160. Max RPM 7000. Crankcase aluminum light alloy. Cylinder head light alloy with hemispherical combustion chambers. Crankshaft on seven bearings one of which is for axial support. Inclined overhead valves actuated through rocker arms from single overhead camshaft for each bank of cylinders. Camshafts chain driven, hairpin valve springs. 3 type 36 DCO Weber carburetors. Ignition by one plug per cylinder supplied by two Marelli magnetos driven from the rear of the camshafts and protruding into the cockpit. The 4 forward speed and reverse gearbox is in unit with the ZF differential. Front suspension is by double wishbones with single transverse leaf spring mounted below and coupled to top wisbone by tubular link. De Dion rear axle with transverse leaf spring mounted below chassis frame, integral Houdaille shock absorbers, De Dion tube located by roller running in vertical guide on rear frame cross member and bronze pad in guide on differential casing. Parallel radius rods run forward to chassis frame from hub carriers. Chassis frame oval section tubular structure. Wheelbase 90 ins. Tread 47½ ins. 2 leading shoe drum brakes.

Luigi Villoresi at speed in the 4-cylinder two liter Type 500 Formula 2 Race Car of 1951

TYPE 500 F-2 (Formula 2) (1951)
2 liter, 4 cyl unblown

4 cylinder in line. Bore & stroke 90 x 78 mm, displacement 1980 cc. Max BHP 170, Max RPM 7000. Crankcase aluminum light alloy. Cylinder head light alloy with screwed-in liners, hemispherical combustion chambers. Crankshaft on five bearings. 60 degree inclined overhead valves actuated through tappets by twin overhead camshafts. Camshafts gear driven. Valve springs coil type. 4 horizontal Weber type 45 DOE single choke carburetors. Ignition by two plugs per cylinder supplied by two Marelli Magnetos driven from the rear of the camshafts and protruding into cockpit. The 4 forward speed and reverse gearbox is in unit with the ZF differential assembly. Front suspension is by double wishbones with a single transverse leaf spring mounted below and coupled to top wishbone by tubular link. De Dion rear axle with a transverse leaf spring mounted below the chassis frame, integral Houdaille shock absorbers, De Dion tube located by roller running in vertical guide on rear frame cross member and bronze pad in guide on differential casing. Parallel radius arms run forward to chassis frame from hub carriers. Chassis fame oval section tubular structure. 2 leading shoe drum type brakes. Wheelbase 86½ ins. Front tread 51½ ins., Rear tread 49 ins.

Engine of the Type 500 4-cylinder Race Car

The Type 375 Mille Miglia "Spyder" with body by Farina

The Type 375 Formula 1 Grand Prix Race Car built for the Indianapolis Race and driven by Alberto Ascari

TYPE 375 F-1 (Formula 1) (1952)
4.5 liter Grand Prix unsupercharged type. Built for Indianapolis 500 mile race.

V 12 cylinder, 60 degree. Bore & Stroke 80 x 74.5 mm, displacement 4,498 cc. Compression ratio 13:1. Max BHP 430; Max RPM 7500. Crankcase aluminum light alloy, cylinder head light alloy with screwed-in liners, hemispherical combustion chambers. Crankshaft on 7 bearings one of which is for axial support. Inclined overhead valves actuated through rocker arms by single overhead camshaft for each bank of cylinders. Camshafts chain driven. Hairpin valve springs. Two plugs per cylinder supplied by single aircraft type magneto driven from front end of the engine. Three Weber type carburetors. Front suspension is by double wishbones with single transverse leaf spring — mounted below and coupled to top wishbone by tubular link. De Dion rear axle with transverse leaf spring mounted below the chassis frame. Integral Houdaille shock absorbers. De Dion tube located by roller running in vertical guide on differential casing. Parallel radius rods run forward to chassis frame from hub carriers. Chassis frame tubular rectangular section side members, circular section cross members and triangulated small tube superstructure. Two leading shoe drum type brakes. Wheelbase 92 ins. Front tread 51½ ins.; Rear tread 51 ins.

Grand Prix Ferraris in action

The Type 212 "Inter" Sports Coupe of 1952

Chassis of the Type 212 "Inter" Model of 1952

TYPE 212 INTER (1952)

Engine V 12 cylinder, 60 degree. Bore & stroke 68 x 58.8, displacement 2562.51cc. Compression ratio 8:1. Max BHP 170. Max RPM 6500. Crankcase aluminum light alloy, with pressed-in cast iron liners. Cylinder head light alloy with hemispherical combustion chamber. Crankshaft high resistance steel counterbalanced, supported on 7 bearings, one of which designed for axial support. Timing inclined overhead valves actuated through rocker arms from a single overhead camshaft for each bank of cylinders. Camshafts driven by slant semi-automatic tensioned chain. Lubrication forced by geared pump, thermostatically controlled oil radiator, filter, and permanently adjusted pressure limiting valve. Three Weber twin-choke type 36 DCF carburetors. Electric starting with ignition key and starter button on dashboard. Single plug per cylinder, 2 distributors and 2 HT coils. FISPA-type membrane mechanical fuel pump. Engine supported on 4 anti-vibration silent blocs.

Clutch Single dry plate type with elastic hub.

Gearbox in unit with engine 5 forward speeds and reverse. Synchromesh on 3rd and 4th gears. Countershaft gear 31/18, gear ratios: 1st 3.157, 2nd 1.946, 3rd 1.403, 4th 1.00, 5th 0.914, rev 4.058. Oil pump and filter are incorporated in gearbox.

Transmission shaft Two piece with sliding joint, incorporates elastic torsional joint.

Rear Axle Fixed type with central casing containing the differential assembly.

Steering with parallel motion independent of wheel oscillation, worm screw drive and helical gear.

Front Suspension Independent with wishbones and single transverse leaf spring, integral rubber blocks, and damping by Houdaille shock absorbers.

Rear Suspension 4 radius rods and semi elliptic longitudinal leaf springs, damping by Houdaille shock absorbers.
Brakes pedal operated hydraulic on 4 wheels, one master cylinder, single brake pump drum type. Hand operated mechanical on rear wheels for parking.

Frame monobloc steel circular section tubular structure. Wheelbase 102 ins. Tread, front 50, rear 49.2 ins. Tires front and rear 6:40 x 15. Dry weight 2200 lbs. Fuel capacity 28 gals.

The Type 250 Mille Miglia Berlinetta Coupe
by Pinin Farina — 1952

The Type 250 Mille Miglia "Spyder" Roadster by Vignale—1952

TYPE 250 MILLE MIGLIA (1952)

Engine V 12 cylinder, 60 degree. Bore & stroke 73 x 58.8, displacement 2953.21 cc; compression ratio 9:1. Max BHP 240, Max RPM 7200. Crankcase aluminum light alloy with pressed-in cast iron liners. Cylinder head light alloy with hemispherical combustion chambers. Crankshaft high resistance steel, counterbalanced, supported on 7 bearings, one of which designed for axial support. Timing, inclined overhead valves actuated through rocker arms from a single overhead camshaft for each bank of cylinders. Camshafts driven by silent chain with semi-automatic tensioning. Lubrication forced by gear type pump, thermostatically controlled oil radiator, filter, and permanently adjusted pressure limiting valve. Three Weber four choke type 36 IF/4C carburetors. Electric starting with starter button on dashboard. Single plug per cylinder, 2 magnetos. FISPA type mechanical fuel pump, and electric supplementary pump. Engine supported on 4 anti-vibration silent blocs.

Clutch Multiple metallic disc type.

Gearbox in unit with engine, 4 forward speeds and reverse, 1st, 2nd, 3rd and 4th synchronized. Countershaft gear 30/23. Gear ratios: 1st 2.536, 2nd 1.701, 3rd 1.256, 4th 1.00, Rev. 2.956. Oil pump and filter are incorporated in gearbox.

Transmission shaft two piece with sliding joint, incorporates elastic torsional joint.

Rear Axle Fixed type with central casing containing the differential assembly.

Steering with parallel motion independent of wheel oscillation, worm screw drive and helical gear.

Front Suspension Independent with wishbones and single transverse leaf spring held by 4 silent blocs and free at the center. Integral rubber blocks, and damping by Houdaille shock absorbers.

Rear Suspension Semi elliptic longitudinal leaf springs, damping by Houdaille shock absorbers.

Brakes pedal operated, hydraulic on all 4 wheels. Two master cylinders, 2 leading shoe drum type, hand-operated mechanical on the rear wheels for parking.

Frame Monobloc steel elliptic section tubular structure. Wheelbase 94 ins. Tread, front &rear 51.1; Tires, front 5:50 x 16, rear 6:00 x 16; Dry weight 1870 lbs. Fuel capacity 40 gals. R-h drive.

The Type 340 "Mexico" Sports Coupe of 1952

The Type 340 "Mexico" Sports Roadster of 1952

TYPE 340 MEXICO (1952)

Engine V 12 cylinder, 60 degree. Bore & stroke 80 x 68, displacement 4101.66 cc, compression ratio 8:1. Max BHP 280. Max RPM 6600. Crankcase aluminum light alloy, with forced in cast iron liners. Cylinder head light alloy with hemispherical combustion chambers. Crankshaft high resistance steel, counterbalanced, supported on 7 bearings, one of which designed for axial support. Timing, inclined overhead valves actuated through rocker arms from a single overhead camshaft per bank of cylinders. Camshafts driven by silent chain with semi-automatic tensioning. Lubrication forced by gear type pump, thermostatically controlled oil radiator, filter, and permanently regulated pressure limiting valve. Three Weber twin choke type. 40DCF carburetors, electric starting with starter on dashboard. Single plug per cylinder, 2 distributors and 2 HT coils. FISPA type mechanical fuel pumps, engine supported on 4 anti-vibration silent blocks.

Clutch Multiple metallic disc type.

Gearbox in unit with engine, 5 forward speeds and reverse. No synchronization. Countershaft gear 31/18. Gear ratios: 1st 3.157, 2nd 1.946, 3rd 1.403, 4th 1.000, 5th 0.914, rev 4.058. Oil pump and filter incorporated in gearbox.

Transmission shaft two piece with sliding joint. Incorporates elastic torsional joint.

Rear Axle fixed type with central casing containing the differential assembly.

Steering with parallel motion independent of wheel oscillation, worm screw drive and helical gear.

Front Suspension Independent with wishbones and single transverse leaf spring, integral rubber blocks, and damping by Houdaille shock absorbers.

Rear Suspension 4 radius rods and semi-elliptic longitudinal leaf springs, damping by Houdaille shock absorbers.

Brakes pedal operated, hydraulic on 4 wheels. Two master cylinders, 2 leading shoe drum type. Hand operated mechanical on rear wheels for parking.

Frame Monobloc steel elliptic section tubular structure. Wheelbase 102.3 ins. Tread, front 50, rear 49.2 ins.; Tires, front 6:00 x 16, rear 6:50 x 16. Dry weight 2,000 lbs. Fuel tank capacity 40 gals. Right-hand drive.

TYPE 342 AMERICA (1952)

Engine V 12 cylinder, 60 degrees. Bore & stroke 80 x 68 mm, displacement 4101.66 cc, compression ratio 8:1. Max BHP 200. Max RPM 5000. Crankcase aluminum light alloy, with pressed-in cast iron liners. Cylinder head light alloy with hemispherical combustion chambers. Crankshaft high resistance steel, counterbalanced, supported on 7 bearings, one of which is designed for axial support. Timing, inclined overhead valves actuated through rocker arms from a single overhead camshaft for each bank of cylinders. Camshafts driven by silent chain with semi-automatic tensioning. Lubrication forced by gear type pump, thermostatically controlled oil radiator, filter, and permanently regulated pressure limiting valve. Three Weber twin choke type 40DCF carburetors. Electric starting with starter button on dashboard. Single plug per cylinder, 2 distributors, and 2 HT coils. FISPA type mechanical fuel pumps. Engine supported on 4 anti-vibration silentblocs.

Clutch Single dry plate type with elastic hub.

Gearbox in unit with engine, 4 forward speeds and reverse. Synchronization on 1st, 2nd, 3rd and 4th. Countershaft gear 30/23. Gear ratios 1st 2.536, 2nd 1.701, 3rd 1.256, 4th 1.000, rev 2.956. Oil pump and filter incorporated in gearbox.

Transmission shaft two pieces with sliding joint, incorporates elastic torsional joint.

Rear Axle fixed type with central casing containing the differential assembly.

Steering with parallel motion independent of wheel oscillation, worm screw and helical gear.

Front Suspension Independent with wishbones and single transverse leaf spring, integral rubber blocks, and damping by Houdaille shock absorbers.

Rear Suspension Semi-elliptic longitudinal leaf springs, damping by Houdaille shock absorbers.

Brakes Pedal operated, hydraulic on 4 wheels. Two master cylinders, 2 leading shoe drum type, hand-operated mechanical on rear wheels for parking.

Frame Monobloc steel elliptic section tubular structure. Wheelbase 94 ins. Tread, front 52.2, rear 51.9 ins. Tires 6:40 x 16 front and rear. Dry weight 2690 lbs. Fuel tank capacity 25 gals. Left-hand drive.

*The Type 553 Formula 2 4-cylinder Race Car of 1953
with Alberto Ascari at the wheel*

TYPE 553 F-2 (Formula 2) (1953)
2 liter 4 cyl unblown

4 cylinder in-line. Bore & stroke 90 x 78 mm, displacement 1980 cc. Max BHP 180. Max RPM 7200. Crankcase aluminum light alloy. Cylinder head light alloy with screwed-in liners, hemispherical combustion chambers. Crankshaft on five bearings. 60 degree inclined overhead valves actuated through tappets by twin overhead camshafts. Camshafts gear driven. Valve springs coil type. Two horizontal Weber 50DCO twin choke carburetors. Ignition by two plugs per cylinder supplied by two Marelli magnetos mounted at front of engine, driven from crankshaft.

The four-forward speed and reverse gearbox is in unit with the ZF differential assembly. Front suspension by double wishbones and transverse leaf spring with rubber block insert between the two wishbones. De Dion rear axle with transverse leaf spring mounted below the chassis frame, integral Houdaille shock absorbers. De Dion tube located by rollers running in vertical guide on rear frame cross member, and bronze pad in guide on differential casing. Parallel radius rods run forward to chassis frame from hub carriers. Chassis frame oval section tubular structure. 2 leading shoe drum type brakes. Wheelbase 85 ins. Front tread 50 ins., Rear tread 49 ins.

Ferrari double overhead cam 4-cylinder engine of 275 horsepower using four Weber side-draft carburetors

The Ferarri version of the "quick-change" rear end applied to the de Dion differential of the Grand Prix cars.

Another version of a Ferrari double-overhead cam 4-cylinder engine. This model having 1985 cc. develops 190 horsepower at 7000 rpm.

The Type 375 "Mille Miglia" sports/racing car of 1953

Chassis of the Type 375 "Mille Miglia" — 1953

TYPE 375 MILLE MIGLIA (1953)

Engine V 12 cylinder, 60 degree. Bore & stroke 84 x 68 mm, displacement 4522 cc. Compression ratio 9:1. Max BHP 340. Max. RPM 7000. Crankcase aluminum light alloy with forced-in cast iron liners. Cylinder head light alloy with hemispherical combustion chambers. Crankshaft high resistance steel, counterbalanced, supported on seven bearings, one of which is designed for supporting axial stresses. Timing, inclined overhead valves actuated through rocker arms from a single overhead camshaft per bank of cylinders. Camshafts driven by silent chain with semi-automatic tensioning. Lubrication forced by gear type pump, thermostatically controlled oil radiator, filter, and permanently regulated pressure limiting valve. Three Weber four choke type 40IF/4C carburetors. Electric starting with starter button on dashboard. Single plug per cylinder, 2 magnetos, two FISPA type mechanical fuel pumps, and one electric pump controllable by dashboard switch. Engine supported on 4 anti-vibration silentblocs.

Clutch Multiple dry plate type.

Gearbox in unit with engine. 4 forward speeds and reverse, synchronization on 1st, 2nd, 3rd and 4th. Gear ratio: 1st 8.44, 2nd 5.66, 3rd 4.18, 4th 3.33. Oil pump and filter incorporated in gearbox.

Transmission Two piece. Incorporates elastic torsional joint.

Rear Axle Rigid type with central light alloy casing containing the limited slip differential assembly.

Steering with parallel motion independent of wheel oscillation, worm screw and helical gear.

Front Suspension Independent with wishbones and single transverse leaf spring, integral rubber blocks and stabilizing bar, damping by Houdaille shock absorbers.

Rear Suspension Trailing link, semi elliptic longitudinal leaf springs. Damping by four twin mounted Houdaille shock absorbers.

Brakes pedal operated, hydraulic on all four wheels. Two master cylinders. 2 leading shoe drum type. Hand operated mechanical on rear brakes for parking.

Frame Monobloc, steel elliptical section tubular structure. Wheelbase 102.3 ins. Tread, front 52.2, rear 51.9 ins. Tires, front 6:00 x 16, rear 7:00 x 16. Weight dry 2100 lbs. Fuel tank capacity, 50 gals.

Type 625 Formula 1 Grand Prix Race Car of 1954

TYPE 625 F-1 (Formula 1) (1954)
2.5 liter Grand Prix 4 cyl.

4 cylinder in-line. Bore & stroke 94 x 90 mm, displacement 2490 cc. Max BHP 230. Max RPM 7000. Crankcase aluminum light alloy. Cylinder head light alloy with screwed-in liners, hemispherical combustion chambers. Crankshaft on five bearings. 60 degree inclined overhead valves actuated through tappets by twin over-head camshafts. Camshafts gear driven. Valve springs coil type. Two horizontal Weber twin-choke type 50 DCO carburetors. Ignition by two plugs per cylinder supplied by two Marelli magnetos driven from crankshaft and mounted at front of engine.

The 4 speed and reverse gearbox is in unit with the limited slip differential housing. Front suspension is by double wishbones with single transverse leaf spring mounted below the chassis frame and attached to lower wishbone, tubular rubber block between lower wishbone and bracket from frame. De Dion axle at rear with transverse leaf spring mounted below the chassis frame. Integral Houdaille shock absorbers. De Dion Tube located by roller running in vertical guide on rear frame cross member and bronze pad in guide on differential casing. Parallel radius arms run forward to chassis frame from hub carrier. 2 leading shoe drum brakes.

Wheelbase 85 ins. Front tread 50 ins.; rear tread 49.2 ins.

*Adjustments during a pit stop.
Type 625 Formula 1 Race Car — 1954*

The Farina-bodied version of the Type 500 "Mondial" Sports Roadster of 1954

Chassis for the Type 500 "Mondial" Ferrari — 1954

TYPE 500 MONDIAL (1954)

Engine 4 cylinder in-line. Bore & stroke 90 x 78 mm, displacement 1984.85 cc, compression ratio 8.5:1. Max BHP 160. Max RPM 7000. Crankcase aluminum light alloy, with pressed-in cast iron liners. Cylinder head light alloy with hemispherical combustion chambers. Crankshaft, high resistance steel, counterbalanced, and supported on 5 bearings, one of which is designed for axial support. Timing by inclined overhead valves actuated through tappets by two overhead gear driven camshafts. Lubrication forced by gear type pump, permanently regular pressure limiting valve, double-bodied scavenge pump with separate oil reservoir of 16 liters capacity, oil pressure 50-60 lbs. Two Weber twin-choke type 42 DCOA3 carburetors, electric starting with button on dashboard, two plugs per cylinder, 2 Marelli magnetos. Engine supported on 5 anti-vigration Silentblocs. Clutch, dry plate with integral circular pads.

Gearbox in unit with differential assembly on rear axle. Oil pump and filter incorported in gearbox. 4 forward speeds and reverse. Gear ratios: 1st 2.25, 2nd 1.5, 3rd 1.108, 4th 1.00.

Transmission shaft Two piece with sliding joint, connected to crankshaft by means of universal joint Fabbri type, and to the gear shaft by an elastic torsional joint SAGA type.

Rear Axle De Dion type with light alloy central casing containing self-locking differential.

Steering with parallel motion independent of wheel oscillation worm screw drive and helical gears.

Front Suspension Independent, double wishbones, transverse leaf springs, integral rubber blocks, damping by Houdaille shock aborbers.

Rear Suspension 4 radius rods and superflexible center pivoted transverse leaf spring De Dion type. Damping by Houdaille shock absorbers.

Brakes Pedal-operated hydraulic on all 4 wheels. 2 master cylinders. 2 leading shoe drum type. Hand-operated mechanical on rear wheels.

Frame Monobloc, steel elliptic section tubular structure. Wheelbase 88.5 ins. Tread: front 50, rear 49.2 ins. Tires, front 5:25 x 16, rear 6:00 x 16. Dry weight 1560 lbs. Fuel tank capacity, 33 gallons.

Type 250 "Europa" Sports Coupe of 1954 — Vignale body

A different treatment by the same body builder (Vignale) of the Type 250 "Europa" Sports Coupe

TYPE 250 EUROPA (1954)

Engine V 12 cylinder, 60 Degree, Bore & stroke 73 x 58.8, displacement 2963.45 cc. Compression ratio 8.5:1. Max BHP 220, Max. RPM 7000. Crankcase aluminum light alloy, with pressed-in cast iron liners. Cylinder head light alloy with hemispherical combustion chambers. Crankshaft high-resistance steel, counterbalanced, supported on 7 bearings, one of which is designed for axial support. Timing, inclined overhead valves actuated through rocker arms from a single overhead camshaft for each bank of cylinders. Camshafts driven by a silent chain with semi-automatic tensioning. Lubrication forced by gear type pump. Thermostatically-controlled oil radiator, filter and permanently adjusted pressure limiting valve. Three Weber twin-choke 36DCF carburetors. Electric starting with starter button in dashboard, single plug per cylinder, 2 distributors. FISPA type mechanical fuel pumps. Engine supported on 4 anti-vibration silent blocs.

Clutch Multiple metallic disc type.

Gearbox in unit with engine 5 forward speeds and reverse. Countershaft gear 31/18. Gear ratios 1st 3.157, 2nd 1.946, 3rd 1.403, 4th 1.000, 5th 0.914, rev. 4.054. Oil pump and filter incorporated in gearbox.

Transmission two-piece shaft centrally supported, incorporating elastic torsional joint.

Rear Axle Rigid type with central light alloy casing containing the differential assembly.

Steering with parallel motion independent of wheel oscillation, worm screw drive and helical gear.

Front Suspension Independent with wishbones and single transverse leaf spring, integral rubber blocs and damping by Houdaille shock absorbers.

Rear Suspension pedal-operated hydraulic on all 4 wheels, one master cylinder, single brake pump drum type. Hand operated mechanical on rear wheels.

Frame Monobloc steel elliptic section tubular structure. Wheelbase 102.3 ins. Tread: front 53.3 ins., rear 53.1 ins. Tires: 6:00 x 16 front and rear. Dry weight: 2320 lbs. Fuel tank capacity, 28 gals. Left-hand drive.

TYPE 750 MONZA (1954)

Engine 4 cylinder in-line, bore & stroke 103 x 90 mm, displacement 2999.62 cc. Compression ratio 8.6 :1. Max BHP 260. Max RPM 6000. Crankcase aluminum high-resistance light alloy, with pressed-in cast iron liners. Cylinder head light alloy with hemispherical combustion chambers. Crankshaft high resistance steel, counterbalanced and supported on 5 bearings, one designed for axial support. Timing inclined overhead valves actuated through tappets by two overhead gear-driven camshafts. Lubrication forced by geared pump, permanently adjusted pressure limiting valve, double bodied scavenge pump with separate oil reservoir of 16 liters capacity; oil pressure 50-60m. Two Weber twin-choke type 50DCOA3 carburetors. Electric starting with starting lever directly on starting motor. Engine supported on 5 anti-vibration silentblocs.

Clutch double plate dry type with elastic hub and Raybestos lining.

Gearbox In unit with differential assembly on rear axle. Oil pump and filter are incorporated in gearbox. 5 forward speeds and reverse. Countershift ratio 25/18. Gear ratios 1st 2.592, 2nd 1.929, 3rd 1.445, 4th 1.099, 5th 1.000.

Transmission shaft two-piece with sliding joint, connected to crankshaft by means of a universal joint with small rollers, Fabbri type and to the gearshift by an elastic torsional joint of the SAGA type.

Rear Axle De Dion Type with light alloy central casing containing the self-locking differential. Klingelnberg bevel teeth gear, and spur gear.

Steering with parallel motion independent of wheel oscillations, worm screw drive and helical gear.

Front suspension Independent, double wishbones, two coil springs. Damping by means of two Houdaille shock absorbers.

Rear suspension 4 radius rods and a super flexible center pivoted transverse leaf spring, damping by Houdaille shock absorbers.

Brakes pedal operated hydraulic on the 4 wheels. 2 master cylinders, 2 leading shoe, drum type. Hand operated mechanical on rear for parking.

Frame Monobloc with tubular elliptic steel structure. Wheelbase 88.5 ins. Tread: front, 50, rear 49.2 ins. Tires: Front 5:25 x 16, rear 6:00 x 16. Dry weight 1680 lbs. Fuel tank capacity 33 gals. Right-hand drive.

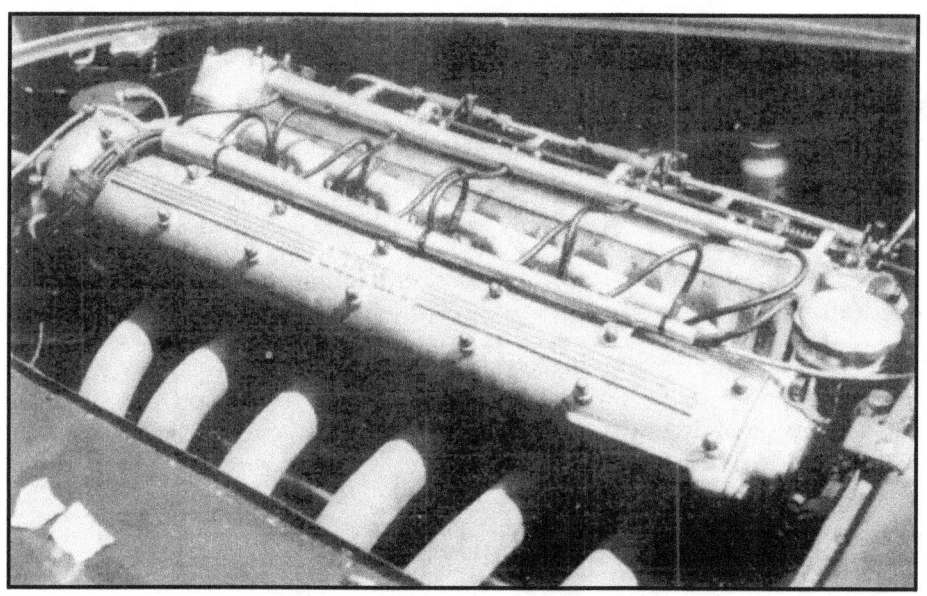

Engine of the 6-cylinder Type 118 "Le Mans" Ferrari — 1954

TYPE 118 LE MANS (1954)

Engine 6 cylinder in-line. Bore Stroke 94 x 90 mm, displacement 3747. 48cc, Compression ratio 8.75.1, Max BHP 310, Max RPM 6000. Crankcase aluminum light alloy with pressed-in cast iron liners, Cylinder head light alloy with hemispherical combustion chambers. Crankshaft high-resistance steel, counterbalanced, support on 7 bearings, one of which is designed for axial support. Timing, inclined overhead valves actuated through tappets, by two overhead gear-driven camshafts. Lubrication forced by gear type pump, permanently adjusted pressure limiting valve, double bodied scavenge pump with separate oil reservoir of 16 liters capacity, oil pressure 50-60 m. Three twin-choke Weber type 45DCOA/3 carburetors. Electric starting with starter button on dashboard, two plugs per cylinder, two Marelli distributors. FIMAC type mechanical fuel pump and Autoflux electric pump controlled by dashbotrd switch. Engine supported on 5 anti-vibration silentblocs.

Clutch Multiple dry plate type with elastic hub.

Gearbox in unit with differential assembly, oil pump and filter incorporated, 5 forward speeds and reverse, Gear ratios 1st 2-78, 2nd 1.96, 3rd 1.4, 4th 1.12, 5th 1.00

Transmission Two pieces with sliding joint, incorporates two Fabbri type universal joints.

Rear Axle De Dion type with light alloy central casing containing the self-locking differential.

Steering with parallel motion independent of wheel oscillation, worm screw and helical gear.

Front Suspension Independent, double wishbones, two coil springs, damping by two Houdaille shock absorbers.

Rear Suspension 4 radius rods and superflexible center pivoted transverse leaf spring, damping by Houdaille shock absorbers.

Brakes pedal operated hydraulic on the 4 wheels, 2 master cylinders, 2 leading shoe drum type, hand-operated mechanical on rear wheels.

Frame Monobloc, Steel elliptic section tubular structure, Wheelbase 84 ins., Tread: front & rear 50.3 ins.; Tires: front, 6:00 x 16, rear 7:00 x 16; Dry weight 1890 lbs.: Fuel tank capacity 40 gallons; Right-hand drive.

TYPE 555 F-1 (Formula 1) (1954)

4 cylinder in-line; Bore & Stroke 100 x 79.5 mm; displacement 2496 cc; Max BHP 250; Max RPM 7500; Crankcase aluminum light alloy. Cylinder head light alloy with screwed-in liners, hemispherical combustion chambers, crankshaft on five bearings, 100 degree inclined overhead valves actuated through tappets by twin overhead camshafts. Camshafts gear driven, valve springs coil type. Two horizontal Weber twin-choke type 58DCOA3 carburetors. Ignition is by two plugs per cylinder supplied by two Marelli magnetos driven from crankshaft and mounted in front of the engine. The 4 speed and reverse gearbox is in unit with the limited slip differential assembly. Front suspension is by double wishbone and transverse leaf spring attached to lower wishbone, the spring being mounted below the chassis frame, with a tubular rubber block between the lower wishbone and bracket from frame. De Dion rear axle with transverse leaf spring mounted above the differential assembly. De Dion tube in front of drive unit and guided by sliding block and twin radius arms forward to chassis frame on each side. Chassis frame small dimension tubing space frame. 2 leading-shoe drum type brakes.

Wheelbase 85 ins; tread Front 50 ins., Rear 49.2 ins. Dry weight 1330 lbs.; Fuel capacity 50 gals.

TYPE 410 MILLE MIGLIA (1955)

Engine V 12 cylinder, 60 degrees, Bore & Stroke 88 x 68 mm displacement 4961.57 cc. Compression ratio 9:1, Max BHP 360, Max RPM 6800. Crankcase aluminum light alloy with pressed in cast iron liners. Cylinder head light alloy with hemispherical combustion chambers. Crankshaft high-resistance steel, counterbalanced, supported on 7 bearings, one of which is designed for axial support. Timing, inclined overhead valves actuated through rocker arms from a single overhead camshaft for each bank of cylinders. Camshaft driven by silent chain with semi-automatic tensioning. Lubrication forced by geared type pump ,thermostatically controlled radiator, filter, and permanently regulated pressure limiting valve. Three four-

Type 410 "Mille Miglia" 4.9 liter Ferrari of 1955. This car led much of the 1,000 Kilometre Race of Argentina

choke type 42DCZ/4C Weber carburetors, electric starting with starter button on dashboard. Single plug per cylinder, Two Marelli magnetos, Two Fispa type mechanical pumps, one electric pump controllable from dashboard switch. Engine supported on 4 anti-vibration silentblocs.

Clutch dry triple plate type with elastic hub.

Gearbox In unit with engine, 4 forward speeds and reverse. Gear ratios, 1st 8.44, 2nd 5.66, 3rd 4.18, 4th 3.33. Oil pump and filter incorporated in gearbox.

Transmission two pieces. Incorporating elastic torsional joint.

Rear Axle Rigid type with parallel motion independent of wheel oscillation, worm screw and helical gears.

Front Suspension Independent with wishbones and single transverse leaf spring, Integral rubber blocks and stabilizing bar, damping by Houdaille shock absorbers.

Rear Suspension trailing link, semi-elliptic longitudinal leaf springs, damping by four twin mounted Houdaille shock absorbers.

Brakes pedal operated, hydraulic on all four wheels, two master cylinders, 2 leading shoe drum type, hand-operated mechanical on rear brakes.

Frame Monobloc, steel elliptical section tubular structure. Wheelbase 104.7 ins.; Tread, front 50, rear 49.2 ins.; Tires 6:00 x 16 front 7:00 x 16 rear. Dry weight 2100 lbs. Fuel tank capacity 37 gals.

The Type 410 "Superamerica," 340 horsepower convertible roadster intended for the U.S. market — 1955

TYPE 410 SUPERAMERICA (1955)

Frame V 12 cylinder, 60 degree, Bore & stroke 88 x 68 mm, displacement 4961.57 cc, Compression ratio 8.5:1 Max BHP 340, Max RPM 6000, Crankcase aluminum light alloy, with pressed in liners. Cylinder head light alloy with hemispherical combustion chambers, crankshaft high-resistance steel, counterbalanced, supported on 7 bearings, one of which is designed for axial support, Timing, inclined overhead valves actuated through rocker arms from a single overhead camshaft for each bank of cylinders. Camshafts driven by silent chain with semi-automatic tensioning. Lubrication forced by geared type pump, thermostatically controlled oil radiator, filter, and permanently regulated pressure limiting valve. Three twin choke type 42 DCF Weber carburetors, electric starting with starter button on dashboard. Single plug per cylinder, two Marelli distributors. Two FISPA type mechanical pumps, and one self-regulating electric pump. Engine supported on 4 anti-vibration silentblocs.

Clutch Dry triple plate type with elastic hub.
Gearbox in unit with engine, 4 forward speeds and reverse, fully synchronized. Gear ratios, 1st 2.20, 2nd 1.153, 3rd 1.252, 4th 1.00. Oil pump and filter incorporated in gearbox.

Rear Axle rigid type with central light alloy casing containing the differential assembly.

Transmission Two piece with integral elastic torsional joint.
Steering with parallel motion independent of wheel oscillation worm screw and helical gears.

Front Suspension Independent, double wishbones, coil springs, damping by Houdaille shock absorbers.

Rear Suspension trailing links and semi elliptic longitudinal leaf springs, damping by Houdaille shock absorbers.

Brakes pedal operated hydraulic on all 4 wheels, 2 master cylinders 2 leading-shoe drum type, hand operated mechanical on rear wheels.

Frame Monobloc, steel elliptic section tubular construction, Wheelbase 110.23 ins.; Tread, front 57.2, rear 57 ins., Tires 6:50 x 16 front & rear; Dry weight 2620 lbs. Fuel tank capacity 27 gals.

TYPE 735 SPORTS (1955)

Engine 6 cylinder in-line, Bore & stroke 102 x 90 mm, displacement 4412.49 cc, compression ratio 8.75:1, Max BHP 360, Max RPM 6000, Crankcase aluminum light alloy with pressed in cast iron liners, Cylinder head light alloy with hemispherical combustion chambers, crankshaft high resistance steel, counter balanced, supported on 7 bearings, one of which is designed for axial support. Timing, inclined overhead valves actuated through tappets, by two overhead gear driven camshafts,Lubrication forced by geared pump, permanently adjusted pressure limiting valve, double bodied scavenge pump with separate oil reservoir of 116 liters capacity, oil pressure 50-60 m. Three Weber twin-choke type 50DCOA3 carburetors, Electric starter with starter button on dashboard, two plugs per cylinder, 2 Marelli distributors. FIMAC type mechanical fuel pump and AUTOFLUX electric pump controlled by dashboard switch. Engine supported on 5 anti-vibration Silentblocs.

Clutch Multiple dry plate type with elastic hub.

Gearbox In unit with differential assembly, oil pump and filter incorporated. 5 forward speeds and reverse, gear ratios 1st 2.78, 2nd 1.96, 3rd 1.4, 4th 1.12, 5th 1.00.

Transmission shaft Two pieces with sliding joint, incorporates two Fabbri type universal joints.

Rear Axle De Dion type with light-alloy central casing containing the self-locking differential.

Steering with parallel motion independent of wheel oscillation, worm screw drive and helical gear.

Front suspension independent, double wishbones, two coil springs damping by two Houdaille shock absorbers.

Rear suspension 4 radius rods and a superflexible center pivoted transverse leaf spring, damping by Houdaille shock absorbers.

Brakes pedal operated hydraulic on the 4 wheels, 2 master cylinders, 2 leading shoe drum type, hand operated mechanical on the rear drums for parking.

Frame Monobloc with tubular elliptic section steel structure, Wheelbase 94 ins., Tread, front 51.9, rear 50.3 ins.; Tires, front 6:00 x 16, rear 7:00 x 16. Dry weight 2000 lbs. Fuel tank capacity 40 gallons. Right-hand drive.

TYPE 857 SPORTS (1955)

Four cylinder in-line; bore & stroke 102 x 105 mm, displacement 3431 cc. Max BHP 280 at 6000 rpm. Compression ratio 9:1. Wheelbase 92.5 ins., Tread, front 52 ins., rear 51.5 ins.

Other details identical to TYPE 750 MONZA of 1954.

TYPE 500 TESTA ROSSA (1956)

Engine 4 cylinder in-line, Bore & stroke 90 x 78 mm, displacement 1985 cc. compression ratio 8.75:1. Max BHP 190, Max RPM 7000, Crankcase aluminum light alloy, with pressed-in cast iron liners, Cylinder head light alloy with hemispherical combustion chambers, Crankshaft high-resistance steel counterbalanced, supported on 5 bearings one of which is designed for axial support. Timing, inclined overhead valves actuated through tappets by two overhead gear driven camshafts, Lubrication forced by gear-type pumps, permanently regulated pressure limiting valve, double bodied scavenge pump with separate oil reservoir of 7 liters.

Oil pressure 50-60 m, Weber twin-choke type 40 DCFA3 carburetors. Electric starting with button on dashboard, two plugs per cylinder, two Marelli distributors. Engine supported on 5 anti-vibration Silentblocs.

Clutch double dry plate type.

Gearbox in unit with engine 4 speeds and reverse synchromesh on all gears.

Transmission shaft two piece with sliding joint, connected to crankshaft by means of a universal joint with small rollers, Fabbri type.

Rear Axle Rigid type with light-alloy central casing containing the self locking differential.

Steering with parallel motion independent of wheel oscillation, worm screw and helical gear.

Front suspension Independent, double wishbones, two coil springs, damping by means of two Houdaille shock obsorbers.
Rear suspension two coil springs and Houdaille shock absorbers.

Brakes Pedal operated hydraulic on all 4 wheels, two master cylinders 2 leading shoes, drum type, mechanical hand brake on rear wheels.

Frame monobloc with tubular elliptic steel structure. Wheelbase 88.5 ins., Front tread 51.5 ins., rear tread 49.2 ins. Weight dry 1510 lbs. Tires: front 5:50 x 16, rear 6:00 x 16. Tank capacity 24 gals.

*The Type 250 "Gran Turismo" of 1956.
Many of this model were sold in the U.S.*

TYPE 250 GRAN TURISMO (1956)

Engine V 12 cylinder, 60 degree, Bore & stroke 73 x 58.8 mm, displacement 2953.21 cc, compression ratio 8.5:1, Max BHP 220, Max RPM 7000, Crankcase aluminum light alloy, with pressed-in cast iron liners, Cylinder head light-alloy with hemispherical combustion chambers, Crankshaft high-resistance steel, counterbalanced, supported on seven bearings, one of which designed for axial support. Timing, inclined overhead valves actuated through rocker arms from a single overhead camshaft for each bank of cylinders. Camshafts driven by silent chain with semi-automatic tensioning. Lubrication forced by gear type pump, thermostatically controlled oil radiator, filter, and permanently adjusted pressure limiting valve. Three Weber twin-choke type 36DCZ carburetors, Electric starting with starter button on dashboard. Single plug per cylinder, Marelli distributors, FISPA type mechanical fuel pumps, engine supported on 4 antivibration silentblocs.

Clutch Multiple disc dry type with Raybestos lining and elastic hub.
Gearbox in unit with engine, 4 forward speeds and reverse, all synchromesh Porsche patent box. Gear Ratios, 1st 2.54, 2nd 1.7, 3rd 1.255, 4th 1.00, Oil pump and filter are incorporated in gearbox.

Transmission two-piece, incorporating elastic torsional joint.

Rear Axle Fixed type with central light-alloy casing containing the differential assembly.

Steering with parallel motion independent of wheel oscillation, worm screw drive and helical gear.

Chassis view of the Type 210 — 1955

Front Suspension Independent with wishbone and coil springs, damping by Houdaille shock absorbers.

Rear Suspension Semi-elliptic longitudinal leaf springs, damping by Houdaille Shock absorbers.

Brakes pedal operated, hydraulic on all 4 wheels, two master cylinders 2 leading-shoe type, hand-operated mechanical on the rear wheels.

Frame Monobloc steel elliptic section tubular structure. Wheelbase 102.3 ins., Tread, front 53.3, rear 53.1 ins.; Tires, front & rear 6:00 x 16; Dry weight 2320 lbs., Fuel tank capacity 27 gallons, Left-hand drive.

The V-12 engine of the 250 Gran Turismo

Close-up of brake, suspension and steering linkage of the 250 G.T. Ferarri of 1955

A variation of body type on the Gran Turismo Type 250 — 1955

Another and somewhat "Americanized" body design for the Type 250 Gran Turismo of 1955

The Pinin Farina "Spyder" version of the Type 250 Gran Turismo of 1955

TYPE 625 Le MANS (1956)

Engine 4 cylinders in-line, Bore & stroke 94 x 90 mm, displacement 2498 cc, compression ratio 9:1, Max BHP 225, Max RPM 6200. Crankcase aluminum light-alloy, with pressed-in cast iron liners, cylinder head light-alloy with hemispherical combustion chambers. Crankshaft high resistance steel, counterbalanced, and supported on 5 bearings, one of which is designed for axial support, Timing, inclined overhead valves actuated through tappets by two overhead gear driven camshafts, lubrication forced by gear-type pump, permanently regulated pressure limiting valve, double-bodied scavenge pump with separate oil reservoir of 16 liters capacity oil pressure 50-60m, two Weber twin choke type 42 DCOA carburetors. Electric starting with either lever directly on starting motor or by button on dashboard. Two plugs per cylinder, two Marelli magnetos. Each suported on 5 anti-vibration silentblocs.

Clutch double dry plates.

Gearbox in unit with engine, 4 forward speeds and reverse all synchromesh.

Transmission shaft two-piece with Fabbri and Saga joints.

Rear Axle Rigid with light alloy central casing containing the self-locking differential.

Steering with parallel motion independent of wheel oscillation, worm screw and helical gear.

Front Suspension Independent double wishbones, two coil springs, damping by means of Houdaille shock absorbers.

Rear Suspension coil springs, axle located by radius rods, and a bracket under the differential, Houdaille shock absorbers.

Brakes Pedal-operated hydraulic on the 4 wheels double master cylinder, 2 leading-shoes, drum type. Mechanical on rear wheels.

The 4-cylinder 225 hp "Le Mans" Ferrari of 1956

Frame Monobloc with tubular elliptic steel structure. Wheelbase 88.5 ins., Tread front 51.5 ins., rear 49.2. Tires 6:00 x 16 front & rear. Dry weight 1770 lbs., Fuel tank capacity 40 gals. Right-hand drive.

TYPE 290 MILLE MIGLIA (1957)

V 12 cylinder 60 degree, bore and stroke 73 x 69.5 mm, displacement 3490 cc. compression ratio 9:1, giving 350 BHP at 7200 RPM. Max RPM 7500. Two valves per cylinder inclined at an angle of 60 degrees. Intake valve diam 35 mm, Exhaust valve diam 29 mm. Two hairpin type valve springs per valve. Single overhead camshaft for each bank of cylinders, chain driven. 3 Weber twin choke 42-1F-4-C carburetors. Two plugs per cylinder with twin Marelli distributors.

Clutch multi-disc aluminum.

Gearbox in unit with differential, four speed and reverse. 1st 2.2, 2nd 1.565, 3rd 1.25, 4th 1.00. Rear axle de Dion. Rear suspension by transverse leaf springs and Houdaille shock absorbers.

Front suspension by wishbone and coil springs.

Chassis Frame, multi tube steel.

Drum Brakes of the two leading-shoe type with two master cylinders and mechanical handbrake action on the rear wheels. Tire sizes, front 6:00 x 16; rear, 7:00 x 16. Dry weight 1880 lbs. Capacity of fuel tank 40 gals. Wheelbase: 92.5 ins., front tread 51.5 ins., rear tread 50.3 ins.

TYPE 315 MILLE MIGLIA (1957)

Engine 12 cylinder V at 60 degrees, Bore and stroke 76 x 69.5 mm, displacement 3780 cc, compression ratio 9:1; Max BHP 380 at 7600 RPM, aluminum cylinder block, twin camshafts for each bank of cylinders chain driven. Six Solex carburetors, two plugs per cylinder, ignition by means of two Marelli distributors.

Gear Box in unit with differential, four forward speeds and reverse. First gear ratio 2.2, second 1.565, third 1.25, fourth 1.00.

Front Suspension coil springs and wishbone, rear suspension De Dion and transverse leaf spring. Shock absorbers Houdaille.

Tubular Chassis Frame, wheelbase 92.5 ins., front track 51.5 ins., rear track 50.3 ins., dry weight 1950 lbs., gas tank capacity 40 gals. Tire sizes: front 6:00 x 16, rear 7:00 x 16.

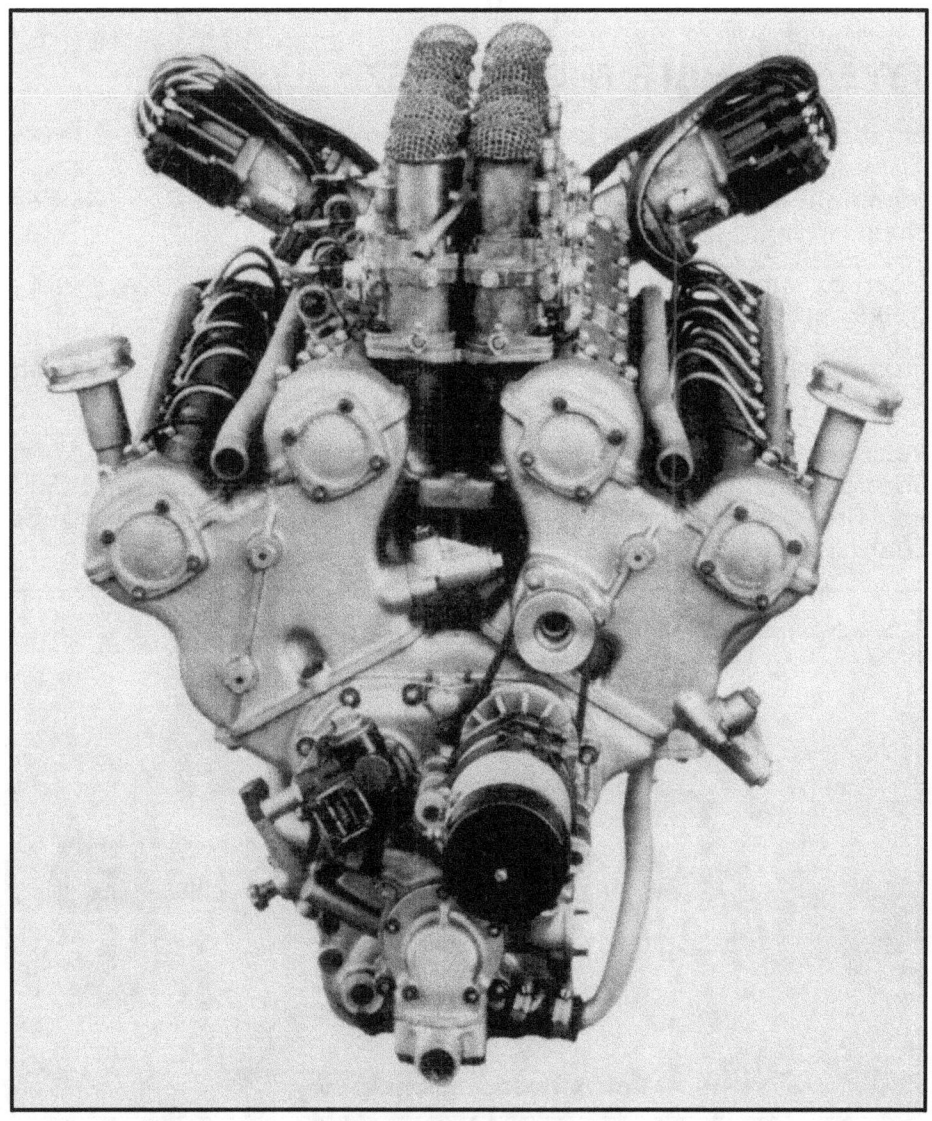

Front view of the V-12 engine of the Type 412

The Type 412 "Mille Miglia" Sports/racing Ferrari of 1957

TYPE 412 MILLE MIGLIA (1957)

Engine V 12 cylinder at 60 degrees, bore and stroke 77 x 72 mm, displacement 4022 cc, Max BHP 447 at 7700 RPM. Block in aluminum light alloy. Twin overhead camshafts for each bank of cylinders chain driven. Six Solex carburetors.

Gearbox and Clutch on rear axle. First gear ratio 0.394, second 0.588, third 0.796, fourth 1.00. Multiple dics clutch.

Front Suspension wishbone and coil springs; Houdaille shock absorbers.

Rear Suspension de Dion, transverse leaf springs and Houdaille shock absorbers. Wheelbase 92.5 ins., front tread 51.5 ins. rear tread 50.3 ins. Tire sizes front 6:00 x 16, rear 7:00 x 16. Dry weight 1930 lbs. Fuel tank capacity 40 gals.

Side view of the Type 412 power plant

A slightly different version of the Type 412. This photo taken during a sports car event in Southern California.

TYPE V-8 F-1 (Formula 1) (1957)

V-Eight cylinder 90 degree. Bore and stroke 76 x 68.5 mm; total displacement 2490 cc. Twin overhead camshaft for each bank of cylinders driven by duplex chain from the front of the camshaft. Two spark plugs per cylinder fired by twin magnetos driven from the rear of each inlet camshaft. Engine angled to left in chassis.

Four twin-choke Solex or four twin-choke Weber carburetors mounted in V of engine.

Gearbox five speed and reverse, first gear serves as starting gear only. Gearbox in unit with differential assembly, clutch mounted on nose of input shaft.

Small diameter tube space-frame chassis, engine no longer forms top frame member, this system replaced by rigid tubes either side.

Front Suspension unequal parallel A arms with ball joint ends and coil springs. Telescopic shock absorbers and anti-roll bar.

Rear Suspension De Dion located by radius rods. Transverse leaf spring and Houdaille shock absorbers. Brakes hydraulic two leading-shoe cast iron linered on alloy drums. Wheelbase 89.7 ins., tread 51.9 ins. Dry weight 1440 lbs. Fuel tank capacity 45 gals.

The car and its power plant — The 1957 Type V-8 Formula 1 Racing Car.

Chassis frame of the Type V-8 Formula 1 Race Car

TYPE 156 F-2 (Formula 2) (1957)

V6 cylinder at 65 degrees, bore and stroke 70 x 64.5, displacement 1489 cc, Max BHP 190 at 9000. Block aluminum light alloy, twin overhead camshaft for each bank of cylinders chain driven. Two plugs per cylinder. Ignition by Marelli bagneto. Three Weber twin choke 38 DCU Carburetors. Five speed gearbox in unit with differential, clutch mounted at rear axle.

Front suspension wishbone and coil springs, Houdaille shock absorbers.

Rear suspension De Dion, transverse leaf springs, Houdaille shock absorbers.

Frame twin steel tube with trussed superstructure.

Wheelbase 85 in., tread 48 in., dry weight 1203 lbs. Fuel tank capacity 40 gals.

TYPE 296 DINO (1958)
(same dimensions as "296 M 1")

Engine V 6 cylinders at 65 degrees, Bore and stroke 85 x 87 mm, displacement 2962 cc. Compression ratio 9:1. Max BHP 316 at 7800 rpm.

Two plugs per cylinder, ignition by two Marelli distributors.

Twin overhead camshafts for each bank of cylinders. Fuel 98/100 octane.

Three Weber twin choke carburetors.

Gearbox and clutch on rear axle, four forward speeds and reverse, first gear ratio 0.394, second 0.588, third 0.796, fourth 1.00.

Front suspension coil spring and wishbones, Rear suspension by means of De Dion and coil springs.

Wheelbase 2350 mm, front track 1296 mm. rear track 1310 mm.

Tires 6.00 x 16 front, 7.50 x 16 rear.

The Type 246 Formula 1 Ferrari Race Car — 1958

TYPE 246 F-1 (Formula 1) (1958)

V6 cylinder at 65 degrees, bore and stroke 85 x 71 mm displacement 2417 cc, Max BHP 290 at 8300 rpm. Block aluminum light alloy, twin overhead camshaft for each bank of cylinders, chain-driven. Two plugs per cylinder. Ignition by Marelli Magneto. Three twin-choke Weber type 42-DCN carburetors.

Gearbox in unit with differential, four forward speeds and reverse, clutch situated at rear axle.

Front suspension, coil springs and wishbones, Houdaille shock absorbers.

Rear suspension de Dion, Transverse leaf spring and Houdaille shock absorbers.

Chassis frame twin tube with trussed superstructure.
Wheelbase 87.4 in., tread 48 in., dry weight 1205 lbs.

Note: The experimental Dino 256 appeared in 1958 fractionally increased in displacement and with Dunlop disc brakes fitted. At Casablanca another version of this experimental car appeared with Girling Disc brakes. This experimental version used coil spring rear suspension with de Dion, and Koni adjustable shock absorbers.

Kurtis Kraft Indianapolis chassis with 12 cylinder Ferrari engine installed

Close-up of Ferrari engine mounted in Kurtis Kraft Indianapolis chassis.

The Type 206 "Dino" Sports/racing Car of 1958

TYPE 312 Le Mans (1958)

Engine V 12 cylinder at 60 degrees, bore and stroke 73 x 58.8, displacement 2953 cc. Max BHP 356 at 8600 rpm. Block aluminum light alloy. Twin overhead camshafts for each bank of cylinders, chain driven.

Gearbox and clutch on rear axle.

First gear ratio 0.394, second 0.588, third 0.796, fourth 1.00.

Multiple disc clutch.

Front suspension wishbones and coil spring, Houdaille shock absorbers.

Rear suspension de Dion, transverse leaf spring and Houdaille shock absorbers.

Wheelbase 92.5 ins., front tread 57.5 ins., rear tread 51.2 ins.

Wheelbase sizes; front, 6.00 x 16, rear, 7.50 x 16.

Dry weight 1770 lbs., Fuel tank capacity 48 gals.

TYPE 206 DINO (1958)

V6 cylinder at 65 degrees, Bore and stroke 77 x 71 mm, displacement 1983.72 cc., compression ratio 9:1, Max BPH 225 at 9000 rpm. Two plugs per cylinder, ignition by two Marelli distributors. Twin overhead camshafts for each bank of cylinders. Three Weber twin-choke 42-DCN carburetors. Fuel 98/100 Octane.

Front suspension coil springs and wishbones. Rear suspension by means of Coil springs, Rigid axle. Four speeds forward and reverse gearbox in unit with engine.

Tire sizes: front, 5.50 x 16; rear, 6.00 x 16.

Wheelbase: 86.5 ins., front tread 49 ins., read tread 48 ins.

Dry weight 1510 lbs. Fuel capacity 40 gals.

Ferrari G-T coupe with body by Pinin Farina

The 375 "Mille Miglia" coupe with body by Farina

SECTION THREE
Precautions and Adjustments

USE OF THE CAR

Basic essentials — The following points should be checked before starting the engine. If the car has been standing idle for some time check the water level in the radiator, the oil level in the engine, the fuel level in the tank and the tire pressures. The carburetor should be cleaned. It will be necessary for the engine to turn sufficiently for the pumps to supply the necessary fuel. The water level in the battery should also be checked.

Starting cold — Pull carburetor choke control fully (refrain from this if engine is warm). Turn on ignition switch key, this must show a red light. Push starter button, and let it go as soon as the engine starts. It is helpful to press in the clutch pedal and not release it while starting the engine.

Starting warm — Do not use the choke when the engine is overheated. Excessive admission of fuel into the cylinders will thus be avoided. On the other hand, it may be advisable to press, very slowly, on the accelerator pedal, ceasing pressure half way through its total run, in order to open the throttle valves thus leaning out the mixture facilitating starting the warm engine. If the engine starts with difficulty, or will not start at all, overhaul the ignition elements; spark plugs and ignition distributor as well as the fuel lines, idling jets, fuel pump and filters.

Before putting the car in motion — A few seconds after starting the cold engine push the choke back to its normal position.

By means of the accelerator make the engine turn at moderate speed, for a few minutes during the summer time, and a little longer in the winter, until the engine is sufficiently warmed up. Full acceleration of the engine, as long as it is not warm must be absolutely avoided.

The oil gauge must show a pressure of 40 to 50 m when the engine is at half throttle.

While the car is in motion — Never allow the car to go beyond the prescribed number of Revs-per-minute (see general specifications). At full speed the oil pressure should not sink below 30m. When the speed, in direct drive exceeds 18.6 mph check from time to time to see that the starting button test lamp is out, which shows that the generator is charging the battery properly. Do not rest foot on clutch pedal when driving. The brake pedal should travel half way, but never more than ⅔ of its total travel for satisfactory braking.

Some possible irregularities and their remedies

Engine will not start — rotates too slowly — Battery requires recharging.

Engine too tight — some bearing jammed or bearings fitted too tightly (if recently overhauled).

Oil too thick — replace with oil of less viscosity of the quality prescribed by the firm.

No spark, or on one row of cylinders only — Control fuses, moisture in the distributors, switch contacts oxydized, dirty or out of order — ground contact switch damaged, or ground wire short-circuited.

Empty Carburetor — Float chamber empty (refill it). Fuel tank empty. Pump damaged. Nipple seats loose. Pump or tank filter dirty.

Fuel arrives at carburetor but engine will not start — Overhaul starter, check and clean idling jets, check for presence of water in fuel, inlet manifold flanges not absolutely air-tight. (Localize air escapes by putting oil on the flanges.) Compression insufficient, due to overwashing of pistons or protracted use of starter (put a little oil in the cylinders). Due to defective tightness of valves or faulty clearances, plugs moist or excessive distance between the points.

Engine does not give full power — Engine does not fire regularly — plugs incorrect type or clearance points too wide. Plugs burnt out — replace with type prescribed. Plug dirty or some wire broken; accelerator does not open completely; valve timing out of order; fuel unsuitable; main jets unsuitable; fuel pressure insufficient.

Loss of fuel from carbuetor — Float perforated; float needle valve dirty.

Engine has been overhauled but not tested on test bench — Valve timing; tappets; ignition timing.

Engine does not work regularly when running at high speeds and plugs are of the prescribed type — Plugs overused; points too wide apart; fluttering of valves due to excessive RPM or to damaged valve spring.

Engine detonates at high speed — Plugs overheated; plug insulator split; overadvance of ignition; fuel not suitable.

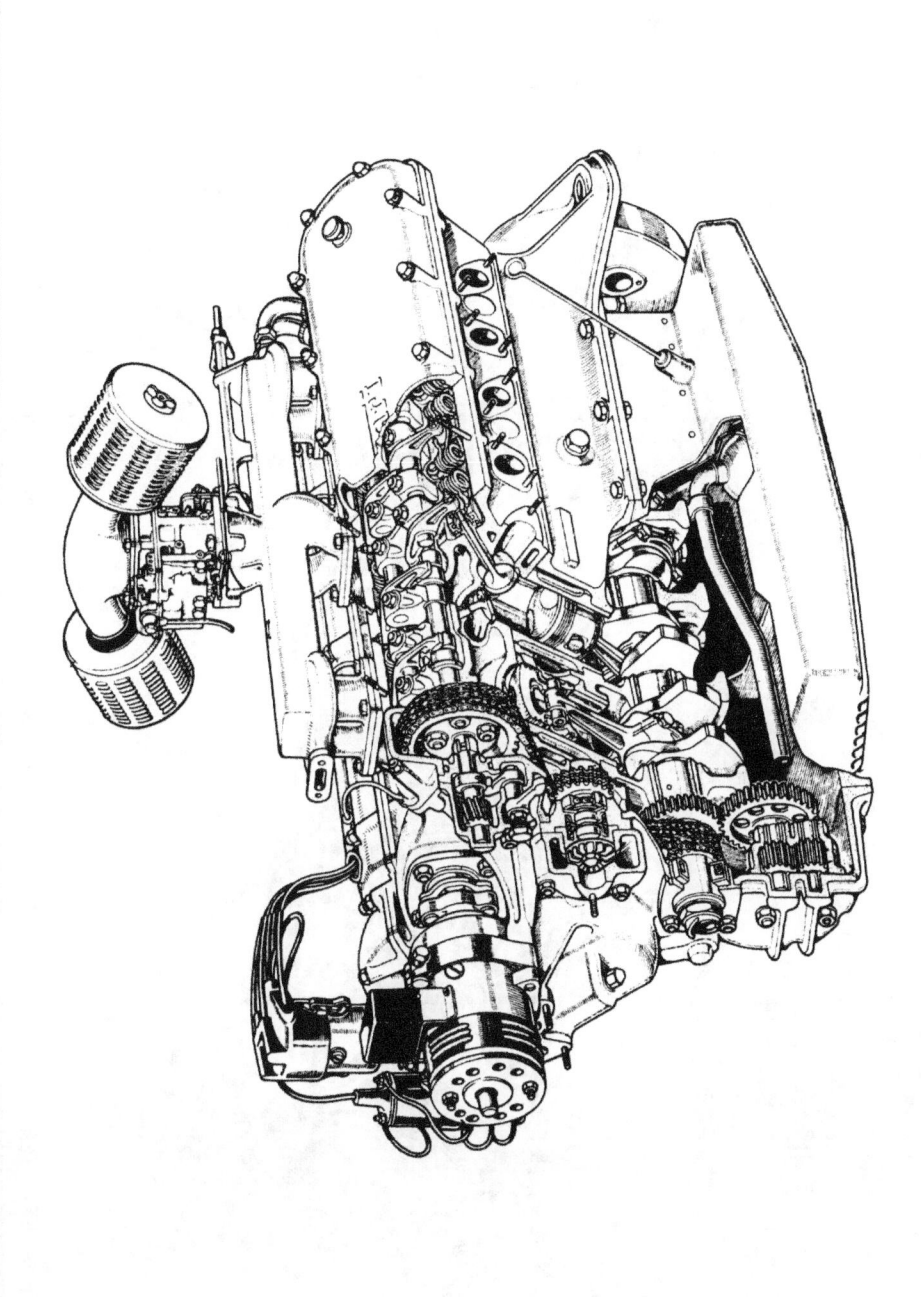

CUT-AWAY VIEW OF THE TYPE 166 "INTER" ENGINE

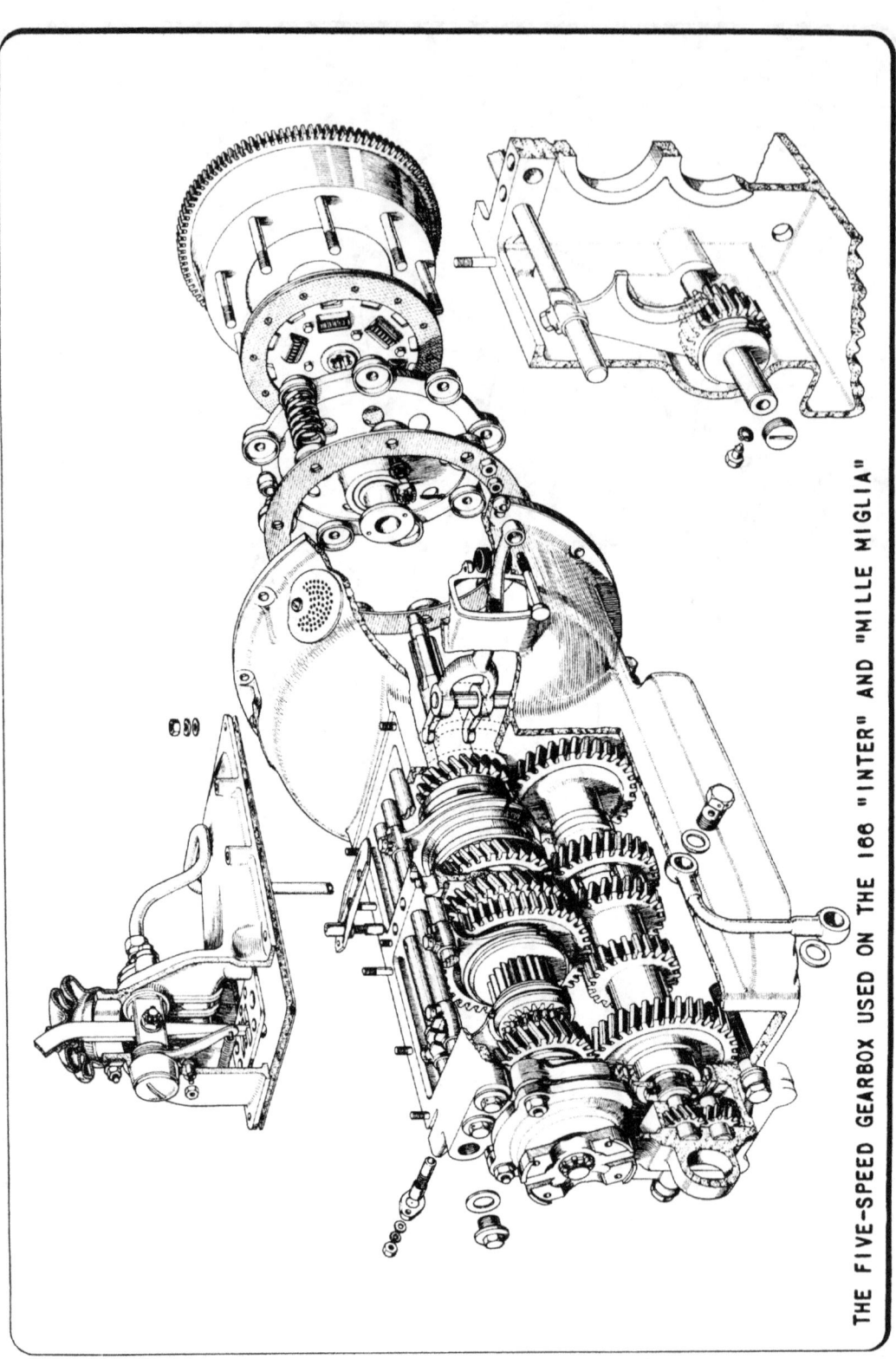

THE FIVE-SPEED GEARBOX USED ON THE 166 "INTER" AND "MILLE MIGLIA"

SECTION FOUR
Maintenance and Tune-up Suggestions

Ignition — adjustment, and eventual replacement of the contacts or the contact breakers of the distributors, should be executed either by the factory or by the authorized agents.

Carburetion — the carburetor adjustments should not be altered and dismantling internal parts is likewise unadvisable. However if necessary to vary the richness of the mixture for slow running, the requisite screws can be adjusted. To enrich the mixture unscrew, and to weaken the mixture the screws should be tightened. The minimum engine running rate is 800 rpm, adjustable by turning the horizontal throttle screws.

Rear axle — to correct the clearance, dismantling of the rear axle is unavoidable, therefore it should be made certain that the necessary tools are available. This operation does not present any difficulties.

Steering — The steering system does not require special care. Eventual clearances between screw and sector may be compensated by removing the box from the chassis, and turning in the required direction the eccentric bushing holding the crown, first taking care to remove the lock washer.

Shock absorbers — the braking effect has been carefully adjusted by the factory, and alteration is not recommended. Should adjustment be necessary, the adjusting pin should be turned in successive steps of not more than ¼ in. in either direction according to the effect required. Two arrows on the shock absorber indicate the direction of rotation. After each 1500 miles remove the filler plug and fill to top with shock absorber fluid.

Clutch — The idle stroke of the pedal should be about ⅜ in. In the case that this clearance should diminish or increase, adjust the relevant screw. The clutch slip might be due to 1) Breakage of lining, 2) Unsuitable or worn out linings, 3) presence of oil on the lining surface. In all these cases a complete overhaul would be advisable.

Brakes — From time to time check the fluid level in the reservoirs located under the dashboard. Replace shoe lining whenever the thickness is reduced to half.

The large diameter drums in light alloy have shrunken-in iron liners fixed with rivets. The types up to the 212 Inter have a single master cylinder, and single pump acting on the brake shoes, the other models have two master cylinders either double in one unit, or two separate cylinders. These models have two pumps acting on the brake shoes.

The brake fluid check should be made every 1000 mi. and substitution of the fluid every 2000 mi.

Before starting — Before starting the engine, check both oil and water levels, as well as the efficiency of the spark plugs; after prolonged periods of activity, first clean the carburetor float chambers and fuel filters, then fill the float chambers with gasoline. This done, the engine may be started either by inserting the ignition key and pressing the starter button, or, in the case of cars equipped with magnetos, by switching on the magnetos and pressing the starter button. In the case of cars fitted with a supplementary electric pump, switch on until the carburetors are full before attempting to start the engine.

In cases where the motor is very hot the starter should not be used, thus avoiding introduction of excessive fuel into the carburetors. The accelerator pedal should be depressed lightly (to half stroke of the pedal) to open the butterfly valves in order to weaken the mixture, which will facilitate starting the motor. If starting still presents difficulty the plugs and distributors should be checked, also the idling jet of the carburetor, the fuel pump, and filter.

Avoid undue acceleration, allow the engine to warm up - - - especially in cold weather. Observe that the oil pressure gauge indicates 40-50m with the engine turning over at medium RPM. The engine will seize if the oil pressure at high RPM ranges falls below 30m.

Observe from time to time whether the luminous gauge in the starter button remains unlighted when the car in direct drive moves at a speed greater than 18 mph which indicates that the dynamo charges the battery regularly. Avoid keeping your foot on the clutch pedal when unnecessary.

To be effective, the brake pedal must run to the middle of the stroke, but it should never exceed ⅔ of its total travel.

Dismantling the engine — A special cradle, on which the engine may be fixed on its four brackets, is indispensable. After mounting the engine on this cradle, draw off sump oil by unscrewing drain plug. Then draw off the water by removing the two drain plugs on the sides of the crankcase.

This done, remove the sump. The carburetors may now be removed. After this the distributors and generator together with their supports and drive pinions may be removed.

The camshaft cover can now be removed, followed by the camshaft retainer caps, and the camshaft supports complete with rocker arms and bolts which attach the camshaft drive gears to the actual shaft.

On the timing chain box at the point of attachment of the distributors, two flanges will be fround of diameter corresponding to the central hole of the camshaft drive gears, from these the camshaft drive gears can be detached, resting them on the flange. The chain must not be removed, it is without joint. This permits the removal of the camshafts, and the cylinder head after having unscrewed the bolts fixing the head to the crankcase, and utilizing a special tool for the purpose. It is now possible to remove the distribution box by removing the chain tensioner, and by unscrewing the nuts and bolts fixing it to the crankcase, including the bolt situated in the inside of the oil filter body, and the nut fixing the oil pump intake tube at the crankshaft support.

To remove the connecting rods and pistons, it is advisable to rotate the cradle through 90 degrees in such a way that the flywheel is at the bottom, thus tilting the engine, after which the two con rod bolts can be unscrewed, after which the connecting rod and piston can easily be removed.

The cylinder liners should never be removed except for actual replacement.

Overhauling the engine — Main and Connecting rod bearings — these are of the Vandervell thinwall type. Neither crankshaft nor bearings if well lubricated are subject to very great wear, nevertheless should the clearances (which on a new engine range from .00118" to .00196") attain .00393", replace the bearings. If owing to wear, the crankshaft requires grinding, use bearings of such diameter as to restore the clearances of .00118" to .00196". Keep both connecting rod and main bearings to the undersizes specified. Never retouch the bearings, lest the special treatment their surfaces have undergone, should be affected.

The clearances between each pair of connecting rods mounted on the same crankpin should be .00393" to .00590".

Pistons — the minimum clearance between pistons and liners should range from .00393" to .00472", the piston being measured from the upper side of the lower scraper ring groove. Should the liner wear measured by comparison gauge, attain .00590", it is advisable to replace it.

The pistons must be totally free from cracks. In order to detect the smallest crack, hold the piston at its upper end, and keeping it suspended between thumb and forefinger, strike the lower end with the piston pin. If the resulting sound is non-metallic, the piston is faulty and must be replaced.

The compression and scraper rings must be replaced as soon as the ring junction aperture exceeds .0236" to .0275". The new rings must have a junction aperture of not less than .3937", and not more than .11811". Both compression rings are to be completely free on their seats.

Valve, springs — Check concentricity of valve heads and stems, and grind seats whenever necessary. Replace valves if badly worn or buckled. Replace all valve springs as soon as they no longer present their original load, as this is a certain sign of cracks or other weaknesses.

Rocker arms — up to type 212 Inter it is sufficient to check the contact surfaces are not marred, from types 250 onwards the roller bearings should be checked for excessive play.

Cylinder head — It is necessary to clean the combustion chamber as well as the exhaust and water ducts; these latter must be freed as far as possible from any chalky sediment. Check the openings of the valve guides, and replace those whose wear exceeds 0.1 mm. Mill if necessary the valve seat. The operation completed, check the seal as follows: 1) screw an undamaged spark plug into each combustion chamber, 2) fill the combustion chamber with gasoline,

3) send a jet of compressed air into each inlet or exhaust duct, and observe whether air bubbles form in the liquid. If this be the case, the valves will have to be reground with greater care, then repeating the test until absolutely no bubbles are formed, indicating a perfect seal.

Cylinder liners — As mentioned before these should be replaced when the liner wear exceeds .00590". For the small motor versions it is necessary to heat the crankcase to 60 degrees Centigrade to replace the liner, taking care that the cold clearance between the new liner and the crankcase seat is .00157" to .00196". After the substitution check to see that the new liners are firmly fixed in the proper seats. It is then necessary to retouch the tops of the new liners as it is imperative that the liners be absolutely equal. For the large engine cars the liners must be unscrewed from the head using a special tool. Be certain to remove all chalky matter from the outsides of the liners.

Oil pump and water pump — these are not subject to a great amount of wear so that overhaul is only exceptionally required. It is, however, possible that the water pump gland packing needs to be replaced from time-to-time. Make certain that the new one fits perfectly, to prevent loss of water.

Distributor, Magnetos and Generator — Their overhaul and repair should be exclusively performed either by the manufacturing firm or by their authorized dealers. This applies to any other part of Ferrari engines not constructed in the Ferrari works.

Assembly of engine — For the small motor types, the first operation is the mounting of the crankshaft, with special regard to the cleanliness of the crankcase and crankshaft. It is essential after fitting the main bearing supports, that the crankshaft be free to rotate. After this the pistons, attached to their respective connecting rods, can be fitted. This can be performed by turning the crankcase through 90 degrees to a vertical position with the flywheel at the bottom; great attention should be paid to the correspondence of the numbers on the connecting rods and their respective cylinders. After closing the connecting rod bolts it should be made certain that the connecting rods are free on their respective crankpins.

For the larger engine types the crankshaft must be mounted after fitting the cylinder head, which is performed after fitting the pistons with their respective connecting rods, complete with compression rings and oil rings. Following this the timing chain casing and its contents can be mounted, taking care first that the three spacers are in position. The chain tensioner must be removed so that the chain can be replaced on the drive pinion from the crankshaft, the tensioner can then be replaced. Before replacing the head, the gasket should be installed.

The first head to be mounted should be the right one looking at the engine from the flywheel side, but this is not imperative as both heads have to be mounted without without the camshafts.

All the nuts of the stud bolts fixing the heads must be screwed down tightly and uniformly (if possible with a torque wrench). It is good practice at this point to proceed by raising the pressure in the water chambers to 3-4 atmospheres, obviously removing the spark plugs from the combustion chambers, turning the engine over, with the heads facing downward. If the mounting operation has been accurately carried out not a drop of water should come out of the spark plug holes nor from the interior of the crankcase nor from around the cylinder head gasket. Having checked for perfect water tightness one can proceed with the assembly of the camshafts.

It is important to point out that the operation of setting up the timing gear requires the greatest attention, because a mistake of even a single tooth, is sufficient to damage the valves, especially in an engine with high compression ratio. On the flywheel there are arrows visible at 60 degrees which represent the top and centers of cylinders 1 and 2. No. 1 of the right line near the distribution box and No. 2 of the left line near the flywheel, always, of course, looking at the engine from the flywheel end. Thereupon bring the dead center No. 1 in correspondence with the reference mark on the cylinder block in the special inspection window, and set the camshaft in operation in such a manner that the mark on it near the wheel centering is in a perpendicular position to the cylinder head surface.

Mount the two rockers corresponding to cylinders 1-6 without fitting the nut-locking device. Thereupon get the wheel to slide from the provisory hub fixed to the distribution box, onto its own centering ring on the camshaft, and note whether the references marked on the wheel correspond to those marked on the shaft. If they do not correspond it will be sufficient to count how many teeth the wheel has to be shifted relative to the chain. Loosen the four nuts which fix the chain tightener of the distribution box to remove it about 0.394" from its own base and, causing the wheel to leave the centering of the camshaft, it is possible to shift the wheel to one side or the other to required extent. When the references correspond exactly, lock the wheel carefully on the shaft, keeping in mind that the flange with the square crankpin, regulating the distributor, must also be fixed in the position indicated on the reference thereof.

Having checked that the references of the shaft relative to the support, and of the wheel relative to the shaft correspond to each other, set the flywheel turning 60 degrees in the direction of rotation of the engine so that top dead center of No. 2 comes in front of the inspection window, whilst top dead center of No. 1 will be exactly in correspondence with the upper dead point of cylinder No. 2 of the left side. Again repeat the operation carried out in connection with right side of the cylinders, viz, assembly of the left camshaft and rocker groups of the extreme cylinders without however, locking them, but merely in order to have a reference as regards the camshaft. Should the reference between shaft and wheel in this case not correspond, push the chain tensioner further, spring the wheel over the chain links, until having replaced the chain tensioner into proper position, it is found that the references correspond. In carrying out the operation of shifting the wheel over the wheel teeth, it is necessary to pay attention that the chain does not jump out of the teeth of the crankshaft pinion. To attain this it is advisable not to move the chain tensioner more than stated.

Having carried out all these operations, one can proceed to block the two groups of rockers on each shaft, checking whether the play between the rocker and valve is .00787" exhaust and .00591" intake, and noting the opening and closing of the valves. If the turning coincidence result as shown in Table 1 with an allowance of 2 degrees they may be deemed exact.

In order to carry out this operation it is necessary to have a graduated disc fixed to the flange of the engine/gearbox connection. If because of stretching of the timing chain due to usage, we find timings different than those listed, it becomes necessary to repeat the checking, following the directions indicated hereunder, beginning from the right-hand row of cylinders.

First loosen all the nuts of the rockers so that the shaft can turn without working the valves. Note from the "registrations" how many degrees the timing has to be altered whether advance or retard, bearing in mind that the minimum timing that can be affected is 4 degrees (on the flywheel) and that in order to secure this it is necessary to shift the wheel with the camshaft in one direction by at least 7 teeth relative to the chain, and in the opposite direction only the camshaft relative to the wheel by 1/5th of a turn. Should it now be necessary to advance the timing by 4 degrees, the wheel and the shaft will be shifted by 7 teeth as regards the chain (that is to say, in the direction of rotation of the engine) because as each shifting tooth of the wheel corresponds to 20 deg 10 (naturally read on flywheel and therefore 21 deg 10 equals 148 deg 10) we get a greater advanced shifting of 4 deg 10 as compared with the one obtained by subsequently shifting in the opposite direction only the camshaft by 1/5 of a turn (720 deg 5 equals 144) should the shifting demanded be of about 8 deg the above operation has to be performed twice.

Having thus checked the exact timing coincidence (plus or minus 2 deg) the operation is repeated on the other set of cylinders. It is understood that the reference signs between wheel and camshaft do not tally any longr and it becomes necessary to make other signs on the wheel, cancelling the first ones. This having been done the rockers are mounted, making certain that after the tightening the nuts, the rockers turn freely on their crankpins. This detail is most important because the seizing of a rocker can cause serious damage to the engine.

To put the magnetos into phase it is necessary to place the dead center No. 1 marked on the flywheel corresponding with the sign on the inspection window, and check that the reference of the cams corresponds with the one of the rocker support near the wheel. This means that cylinder No. 1 is in combustion phase. This done, the flywheel is turned by 10 degrees in the opposite direction of the rotation, the magneto (or distributor) are thereupon pegged by means of the distributing brush in position 1 and also the make-and-break small points just when they appear to open (use special small blade or thin paper). Once the flywheel has been moved by 60 degrees in the direction of the run, the same operation is repeated for setting the second magneto or distributor.

Gearbox — Dismantling. The first operation to be performed is to remove the small upper cap, the universal joint and small fork fitted on to the driving shaft. Then remove the small rear cap and the small forward cover which carries the clutch disengaging lever. Then unscrew the forward ring of the secondary shaft and push the shaft out of the forward ball bearings until the fixed transmission gear falls to the bottom of the box. Only then will it be possible to untwist the transmission gear chuck without danger of spoiling the synchronizer of the direct drive. Having subsequently removed the nut which locks the synchronizer protecting sleeve on to the propeller shaft one can proceed with the dismantling of all the separate items without difficulty.

LUBRICATION

Engine — For engine lubrication the oil should not drop below the minimum level nor exceed the maximum level. At maximum the oil content in the sump is 7 liters for the 212 Inter and the 250 Mille Miglia, and 6.5 liters for the 340 Mille Miglia and 342 America. When the oil is warm and the engine is running at maximum speed, pressure should never sink below 30 meters, the normal working pressure is 50 meters.

Gearbox — Lubrication is provided for by means of a geared pump and filter.

Leaf Springs — In order to keep front and rear leaf springs in perfect working condition and eliminate noise, leaf springs should be washed every 620 to 930 miles with gasoline. A little graphited oil should be injected by means of a syringe between the leaves after lifting the car off the ground with a jack applied to the central part of the leaf springs, and removing the small bolts of the spring clips. Care should be taken to replace the bolts correctly.

Valve Clearance — These clearances should be checked every 2000 miles. Inlet .00591", exhaust .00787".

Ignition — Regulation and replacement of the contact points of the distributors should be exclusively effected by the manufacturing firm or by workshops authorized by the manufacturer. Spark plugs recommended are Marchal 32/2H, Marelli CW 240, Lodge RL 47, or Champion NA 10 which should be replaced every 5,000 to 6,200 miles. The normal clearance for plug points is .0118" - .0157"

Carburetor — This should not be taken apart nor the settings altered. The mixture may be varied at will by means of the inclined adjusting screws. To make the mixture richer—unscrew, to make it weaker tighten screw. Minimum idling speed 800 RPM. Throttle governed by means of opposite horizontal screws.

Rear Axle — To take up any play it is necessary to dismantle the axle.

Steering unit — This does not require special attention. Any play between cam and sector may be adjusted by taking the box out of the frame and rotating the eccentric sleeve carrying the sector, in the direction required, after removing the clamping plates. The box should be kept full of thick oil, which may be done by removing the top cover.

Shock absorbers — Every 1500 miles remove the reservoir cap of each shock absorber and replenish.

Clutch — The clutch pedal, in proper working condition, should run clear for about 0.394" before acting on the clutch throw-out sleeve. If the clutch shows a tendency to slip it is necessary to ascertain:
1) That the pedal runs as prescribed above, if not adjust the proper regulator.
2) That there is neither oil nor other greasy substance on the lining surfaces.
3) That there is no broken lining.
4) That the linings are neither overworn nor of the wrong quality.

When overhauling the clutch, do not forget to insert a little heat-proof grease into the throw-out ball-bearing. When reassembling the parts, take care to replace the pin or bolt and nuts in their right positions in order not to alter the spring load.

In good working conitions, the clutch ought to present the following characteristics:
1) The clearance between the clutch thrust bearing and the small throw-out levers should be of 0.118" to 0.157". In this condition the clutch pedal has a free stroke of above 0.393".
2) The tablet surfaces should be perfectly smooth and lying parallel to each other.
3) The surfaces of the pressure plate, friction plate and bell housing should also be perfectly smooth and level.
4) Contact surfaces of the tablets and discs should be absolutely free from grease or oil.
5) The clutch thrust bearing should be lubricated with heat-resisting grease.

Newly mounted tablets are 0.315" thick.

Amount of wear should not exceed 0.078". Beyond this limit the tablets should be replaced.

Compensate for the increase of clearance due to wear of the tablets by the special adjusting device.

Oliver Gendebien at speed.

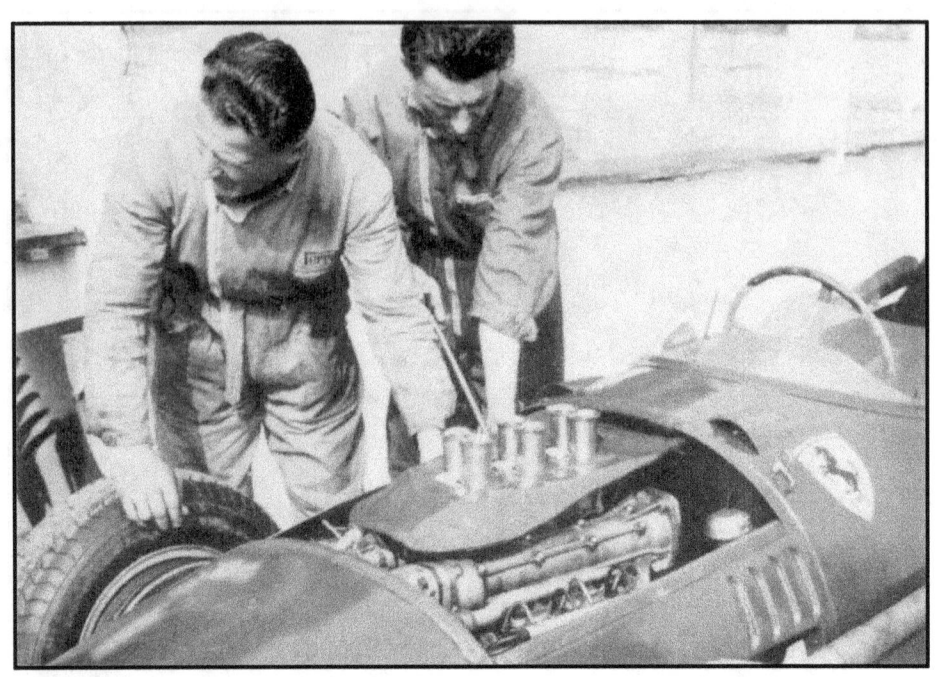

The Type 246 Formula 1 Ferrari race car of 1956 utilizing the 2417 cc. V-6 double overhead cam engine.

Close-up of the V-6 Type 246 Engine

SECTION FIVE
Valve Timing and Carburetor Adjustments

TABLE 1 — TIMING

	212 Inter	250 Mille Miglia
Intake		
opening advance	20 deg	22 deg
closing retard	55 deg	66 deg
Exhaust		
opening advance	60 deg	67 deg
closing retard	15 deg	17 deg
	340 Mexico	**342 America**
Intake		
opening advance	24 deg	25 deg
closing retard	68 deg	55 deg
Exhaust		
opening advance	70 deg	58 deg
closing retard	20 deg	14 deg
	340 Mille Miglia	
Intake		
opening advance	24 deg	
closing retard	68 deg	
Exhaust		
opening advance	70 deg	
closing retard	20 deg	

TABLE 2 — TIMING

	500 Mondial	750 Monza
Intake		
opening advance	35 deg	50 deg
closing retard	80 deg	80 deg
Exhaust		
opening advance	80 deg	78 deg
closing retard	30 deg	48 deg
Carburetors	**500 Mondial**	**750 Monza**
type	Weber 40DCOA3	Weber 50DCOA3
chokes	36 mm	44 mm
main jets	1.9 mm	2.5 mm
air brakes	2.25 mm	2.5 mm
bowl	F2 type	F2 type
idle jets	0.8 mm	1.0 mm
pump jets	0.5 mm	0.5 mm
pump stroke	4 mm	4 mm

TABLE 3 — TIMING
3.7 Litre and 4.4 Litre

Intake	
opening advance	50 deg
closing retard	80 deg
Exhaust	
opening advance	78 deg
closing retard	48 deg
Carburetors	
type	Weber 50 DCOA3
chokes	40 mm
main jets	1.75
air brakes	1.40
bowl type	F 2
idle jets	0.8
pump jets	0.5
pump stroke	4 mm

SECTION SIX
Acceleration times

Acceleration tests

MPH	Type 212 Seconds	Type 250 Seconds	Type 340 Seconds	Type 375 Seconds
0 - 40	5	3.5	4	3.1
0 - 60	7	5	6	4
0 - 70	9	6	8	5.5
0 - 90	14	10.5	12.5	9
0 - 100	19	12.5	16	11.5
0 - 110	24	17	20	13.5
0 - 120	31	23	25	18.0

Type 212 Inter

Speeds attainable at 6500 rpm with 6.40 x 15 tires mph

Rear Axle Ratio	1st	2nd	3rd	4th	5th	4th x 1000 rpm
8/40	33.5	55.0	75.0	105.5	115.5	26.10
9/42	36.0	58.0	80.5	113.0	123.5	28.00

Type 250 Mille Miglia

Speeds attainable at 7200 rpm with 6.00 x 16 tires mph

Rear Axle Ratio	1st	2nd	3rd	4th	4th x 1000 rpm
9/40	50.5	75.5	102.5	129.0	
10/40	56.5	84.0	114.5	143.5	
11/40	62.0	93.15	126.0	157.5	

Type 340 Mexico

Speeds attainable at 6600 rpm with 6.50 x tires mph

Rear Axle Ratio	1st	2nd	3rd	4th	5th	4th x 1000 rpm
10/40	40.0	65.0	90.5	127.0	139.0	
11/40	44.0	71.5	99.5	139.5	153.0	
12/42	50.5	82.0	114.0	160.0	175.0	

Type 342 America

Speeds attainable at 5000 rpm with 6.40 x 15 tires mph

Rear Axle Ratio	1st	2nd	3rd	4th	4th x 1000 rpm
10/40	40.0	59.0	80.5	104.5	
12/42	45.0	67.5	92.0	115.5	

Type 250 Grand Turismo

Speeds attainable with 6.00 x 16 tires mph

Rear Axle Ratio	1st	2nd	3rd	4th	4th x 1000
7/32	54	76	102	126	18
8/34	58	82	110	135	20
9/34	65	92	124	153	22
9/33	67	95	128	157	23

Type 375 Plus

Speeds attainable with 7.50 x 18 tires mph

Rear Axle Ratio	1st	2nd	3rd	4th
13/51x15/16-4.185	73.2	92.5	130.4	162.3
16/48x13/16-3.692	83.21	104.3	145.9	182.2
16/48x15/16-3.2	96.25	118.85	174.7	210.2

Type 750 Monza

Speeds attainable at 6000 engine rpm with 6.00 x 16 tires mph

Rear Axle Ratio	1st	2nd	3rd	4th	5th	5th x 1000 rpm
12/52x20/20-4.34	43	59	78	103	113	18.95
13/55x20/20-3.92	48	65	86	114	125	20.94
14/50x20/20-3.57	52	71	95	125	137	23.00
15/49x20/20-3.26	57	78	103	137	151	25.17
16/48x20/20-3.00	63	85	112	149	164	27.34

With 6.50 x 16 tires these speeds are increased 1.73%

Type 500 Mondial

Speeds attainable at 7000 engine rpm with 6.00 x 16 tires mph

Rear Axle Ratio	1st	2nd	3rd	4th	5th	5th x 1000 rpm
14/50x12/17-5.06	43	59	78	103	113	16.28
12/52x20/21-4.55	48	65	87	114	126	18.02
12/52x20/20-4.34	50	68	91	120	132	18.95
13/51x20/21-4.12	53	72	95	126	139	19.88
13/51x20/20-3.92	56	75	100	133	146	20.94

Type 250 Testa Rossa

Speeds attainable at 7200 rpm with 6.00 x 16 tires mph

Rear Axle Ratio	1st	2nd	3rd	4th
7/34	56	78	103	123
7/32	56	81	109	131
8/34	60	89	117	140
8/32	64	94	124	149
9/34	68	99	132	158
9/32	76	106	140	167

Type 412 MM 4.1 liter four cam

Speeds attainable at 7000 rpm with 7.00 x 16 tires mph

Rear Axle	1st	2nd	3rd	4th
14/16	49	72	98	124
10/43 15/15	56	83	112	141
10/43 15/15 11/42	63	94	126	159
15/15 12/41	70	104	141	177

Type 250 Gran Turismo 1958
Speeds attainable at 7000 rpm with 6.00 x 16 rear tires mph

Rear Axle Ratio	1st	2nd	3rd	4th
7/34 = 4,858	46.6	69.6	93.8	118
7/32 = 4,57	49.7	74	100	125.5
8/34 = 4,25	53.5	79.5	107.5	135.8
8/32 = 4	56.5	84.5	114.3	143.6
9/34 = 3,778	60.3	89.5	121.2	152.2
9/32 = 3,666	62.1	92	124.3	156.6

Type 250 Gran Turismo 1959
Speeds attainable at 7000 rpm with 6.00 x 16 tires mph

Rear axle	1st	2nd	3rd	4th
7/32	53	76	102	125
8/34	58	81	109	135
8/32	61	84	114	143
9/34	64	92	123	152
9/33	66	94	127	156

Strictly for carburetion afficionados. Three dual Webers aid the breathing of this V-12 power plant

----- whereas six (count them) dual-throat pots gulp petrol to motivate this V-12.

Engine testing room of the Ferrari plant showing banks of dynamometers used in checking engine output.

Final assembly section of Ferrari plant for equipment devoted to competition.

Portion of the Ferrari plant devoted to body and chassis assembly. Chassis frames fabricated on left-hand line.

View of multiple heavy machining operations in the building of Ferrari automobiles

Banks of machine tools utilized in fabricating parts for Ferrari engines and chassis

Moulding room of the Ferrari foundry where the many castings for Ferrari engines are manufactured.

Exterior view of the main entrance to the Ferrari factory at Maranello, Italy.

Another view of the exterior of the large Ferrari main building

SECTION SEVEN
Detail Components Drawings, Wiring Diagrams, Lubrication Charts, Brake adjustment Schematics, and Exploded views

Following are detailed drawings of major and minor components of many models of Ferraris, including brake schematics, lubrication and greasing instructions, exploded views of complicated assemblies, wiring diagrams, and complete electrical system schematics.

The 2.7 litre V-12 Ferrari sports car. Only a limited number of these, as interim models between the 2.5 and the 3 litre, were built. Photographed on Modena circuit.

CARBURETOR

(1) Fuel filter
(2) Idling jet screw
(3) Main jet screw
(4) Throttle opening screw
(5) Idling mixture screw

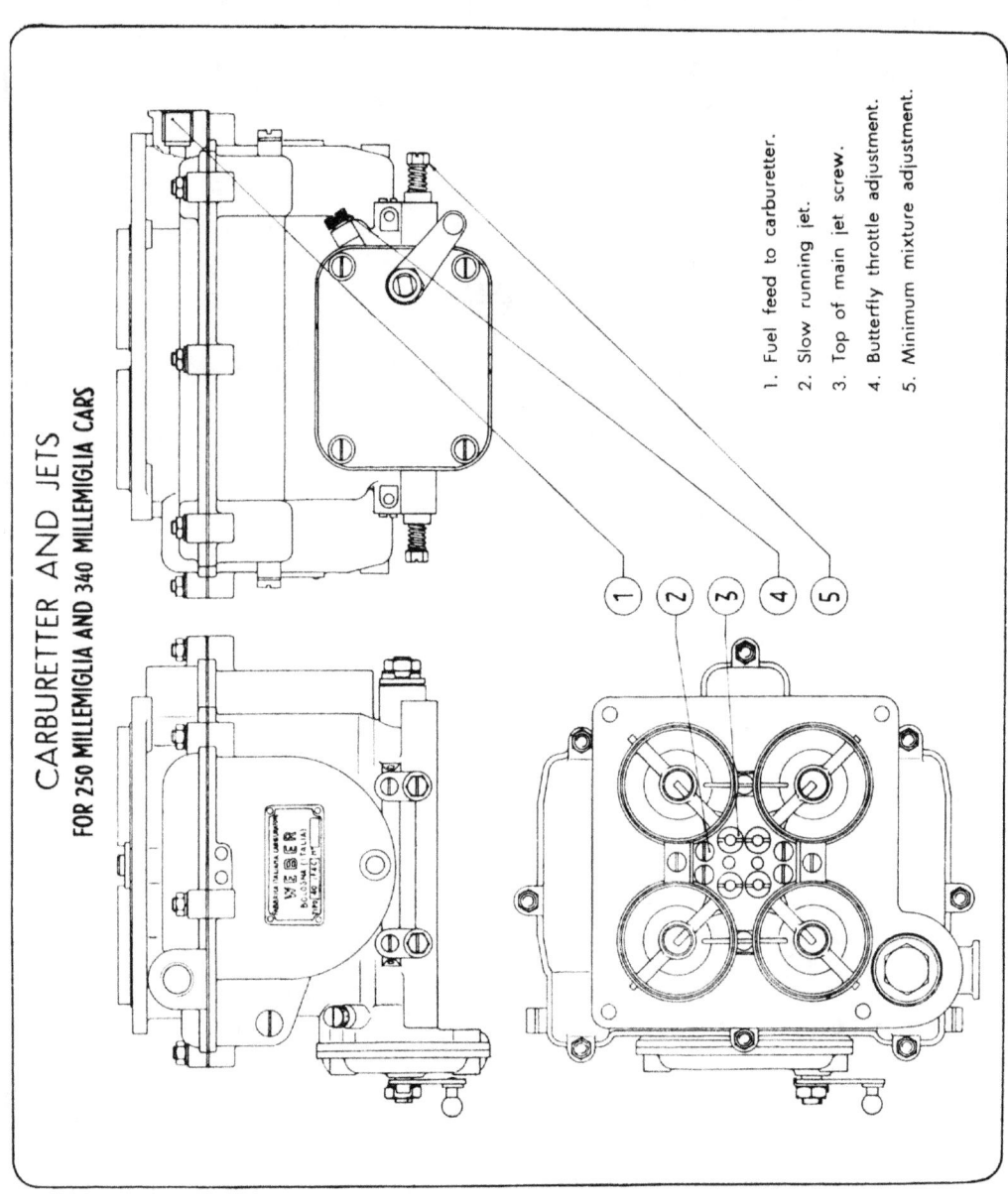

CARBURETTER AND JETS
FOR 212 INTER - 342 AMERICA CARS

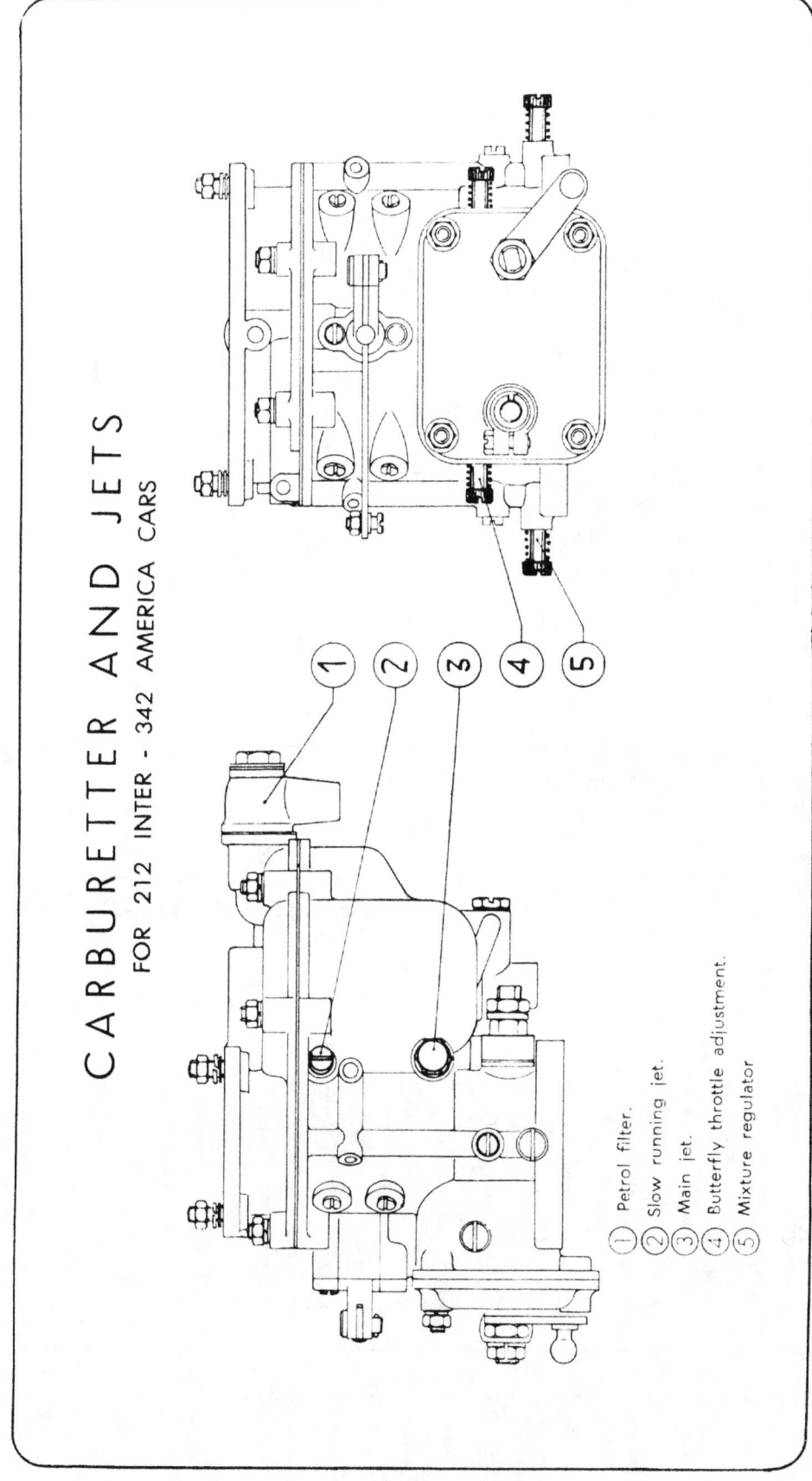

1. Petrol filter.
2. Slow running jet.
3. Main jet.
4. Butterfly throttle adjustment.
5. Mixture regulator

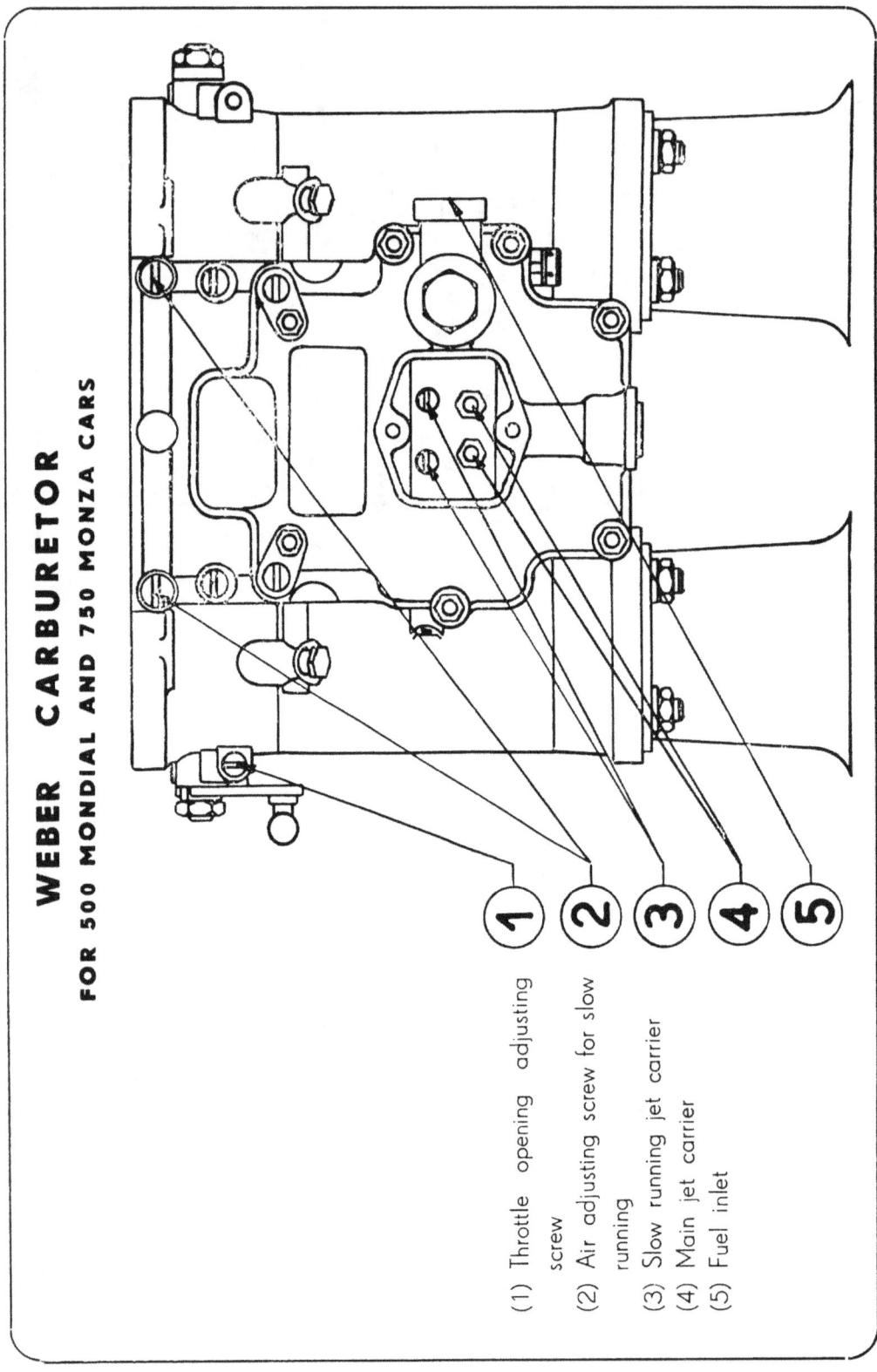

WEBER CARBURETOR
FOR 500 MONDIAL AND 750 MONZA CARS

(1) Throttle opening adjusting screw
(2) Air adjusting screw for slow running
(3) Slow running jet carrier
(4) Main jet carrier
(5) Fuel inlet

PERSPECTIVE VIEW OF TRANSMISSION

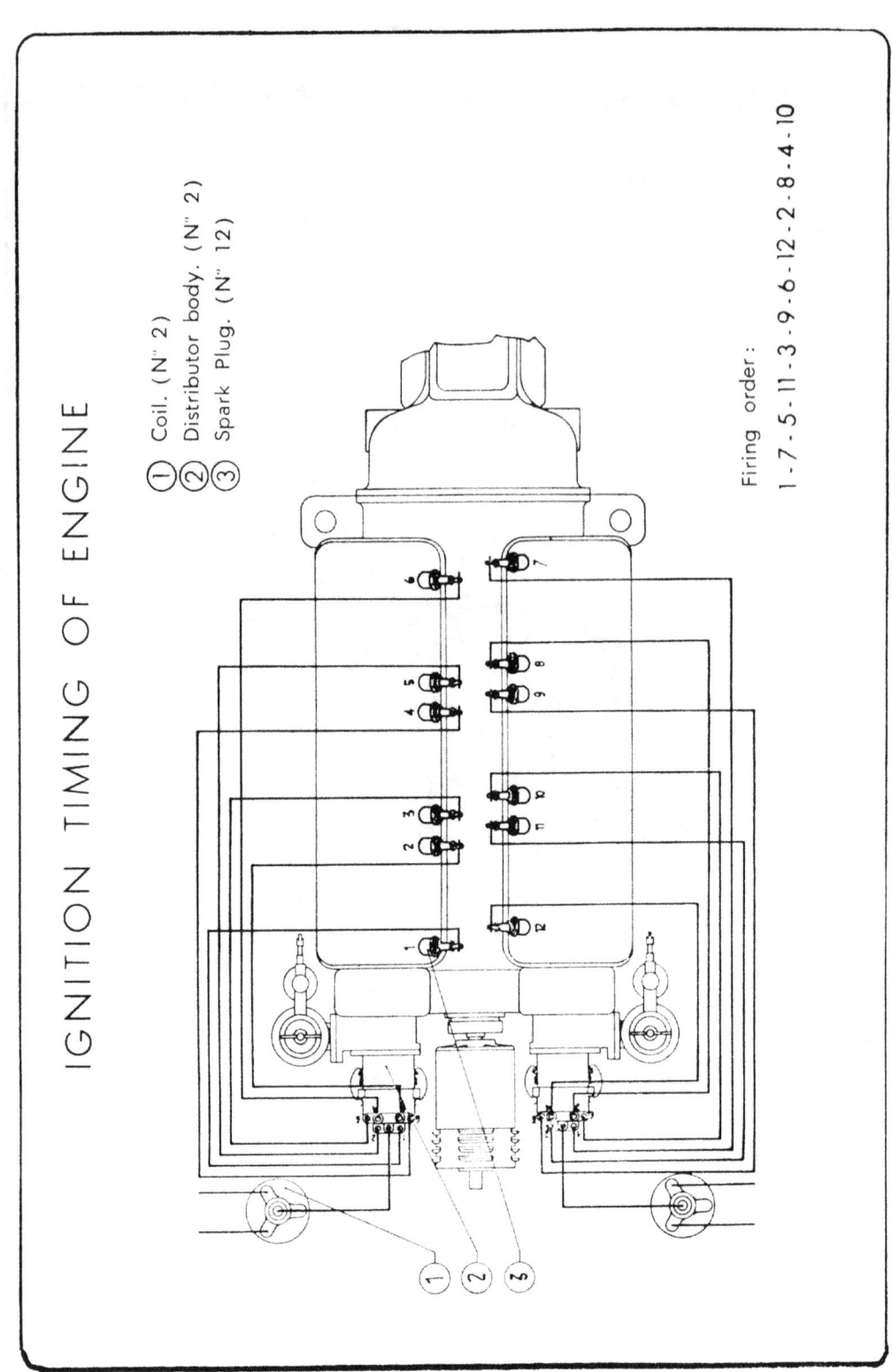

IGNITION TIMING OF ENGINE

① Coil. (N° 2)
② Distributor body. (N° 2)
③ Spark Plug. (N° 12)

Firing order:
1 - 7 - 5 - 11 - 3 - 9 - 6 - 12 - 2 - 8 - 4 - 10

CYLINDER IGNITION ORDER

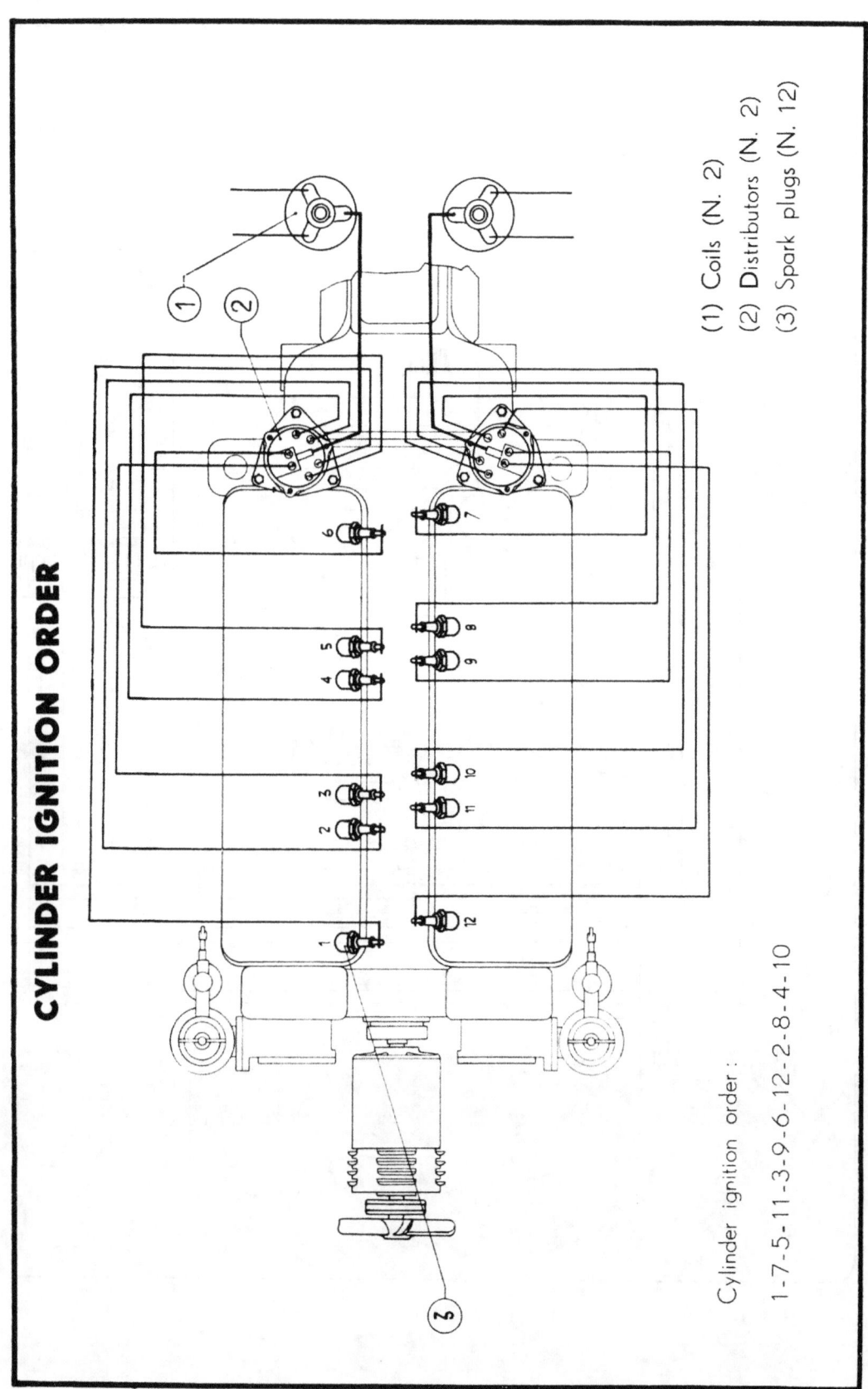

(1) Coils (N. 2)
(2) Distributors (N. 2)
(3) Spark plugs (N. 12)

Cylinder ignition order:

1-7-5-11-3-9-6-12-2-8-4-10

ELECTRIC

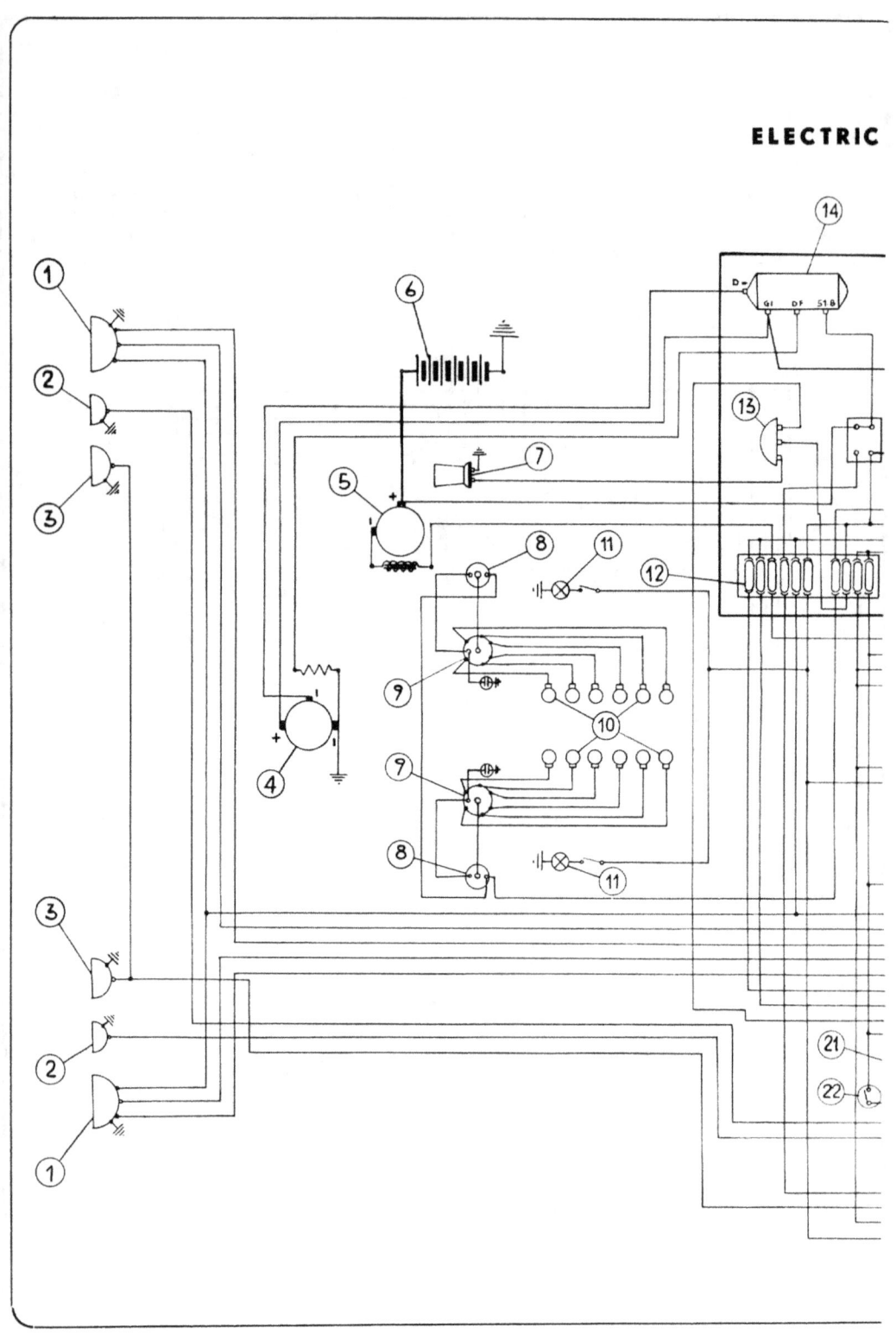

EQUIPMENT

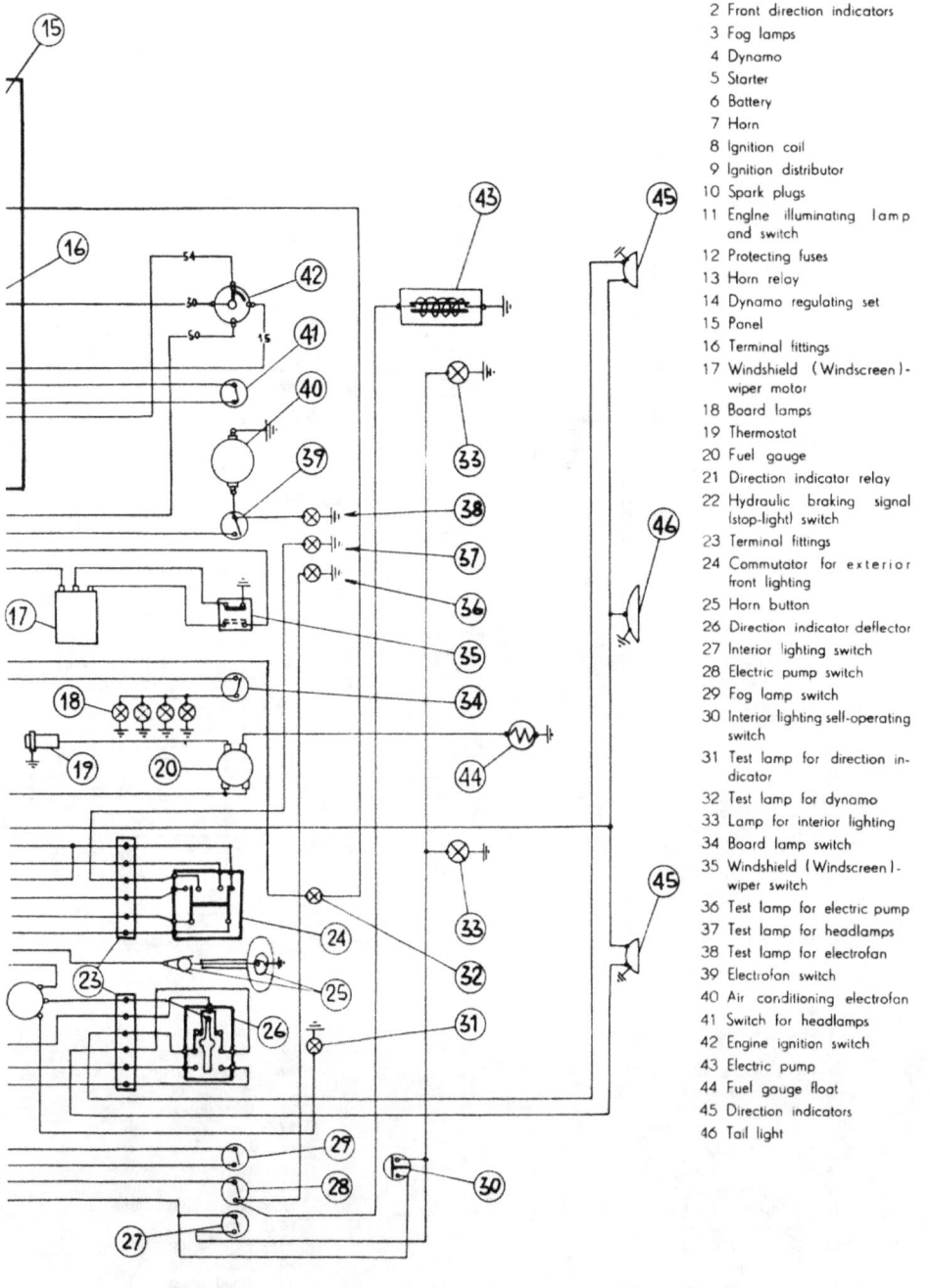

1. Full light headlamps, anti-dazzle, and parking lights
2. Front direction indicators
3. Fog lamps
4. Dynamo
5. Starter
6. Battery
7. Horn
8. Ignition coil
9. Ignition distributor
10. Spark plugs
11. Engine illuminating lamp and switch
12. Protecting fuses
13. Horn relay
14. Dynamo regulating set
15. Panel
16. Terminal fittings
17. Windshield (Windscreen)-wiper motor
18. Board lamps
19. Thermostat
20. Fuel gauge
21. Direction indicator relay
22. Hydraulic braking signal (stop-light) switch
23. Terminal fittings
24. Commutator for exterior front lighting
25. Horn button
26. Direction indicator deflector
27. Interior lighting switch
28. Electric pump switch
29. Fog lamp switch
30. Interior lighting self-operating switch
31. Test lamp for direction indicator
32. Test lamp for dynamo
33. Lamp for interior lighting
34. Board lamp switch
35. Windshield (Windscreen)-wiper switch
36. Test lamp for electric pump
37. Test lamp for headlamps
38. Test lamp for electrofan
39. Electrofan switch
40. Air conditioning electrofan
41. Switch for headlamps
42. Engine ignition switch
43. Electric pump
44. Fuel gauge float
45. Direction indicators
46. Tail light

ELECTRICAL

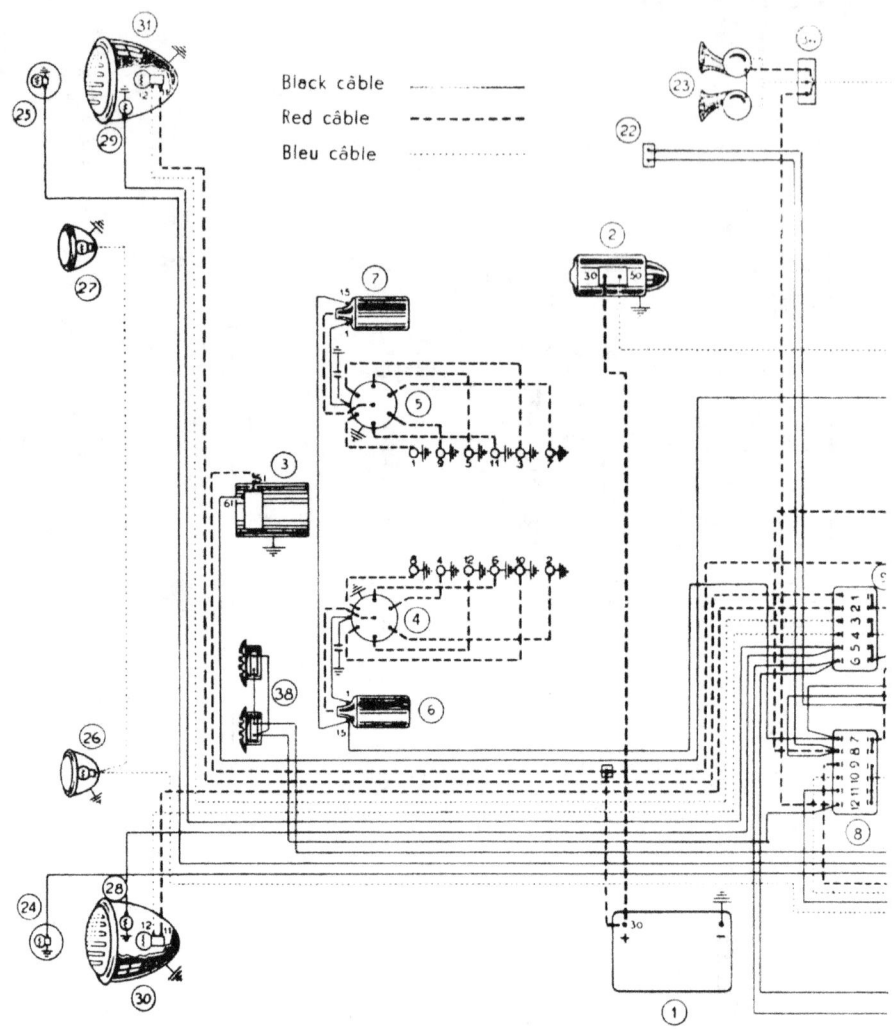

Black cable ————
Red cable — — — —
Bleu cable ·········

1. - Accumulator.
2. - Self-starter.
3. - Dynamo, and regulator.
4. - Distributor.
5. - Distributor.
6. - High tension coil.
7. - High tension coil.
8. - Six point fuse box.
9. - Six point fuse box.
10. - Trafficator switch.
11. - Ignition switch.
12. - Starter solenoid.
13. - Petrol gauge.
14. - Switch for interior light.
15. - Switch for interior light.
16. - Interior lights (rear).
17. - Windscreen wipers.
18. - Tank connection for fuel indicator.
19. - Map reading light.
20. - Dipper switch.
21. - Horn button.
22. - Stop lights.
23. - Horn connections.
24. - Right hand indicator.
25. - Left hand indicator.
26. - Fog or pass light.
27. - Fog or pass light.
28. - Parking light.
29. - Parking light.
30. - Head lamp.
31. - Head lamp.
32. - Stop light control box.
33. - Magnetic dipper for head lamp.
34. - Relay connection for horn.

DIAGRAM.

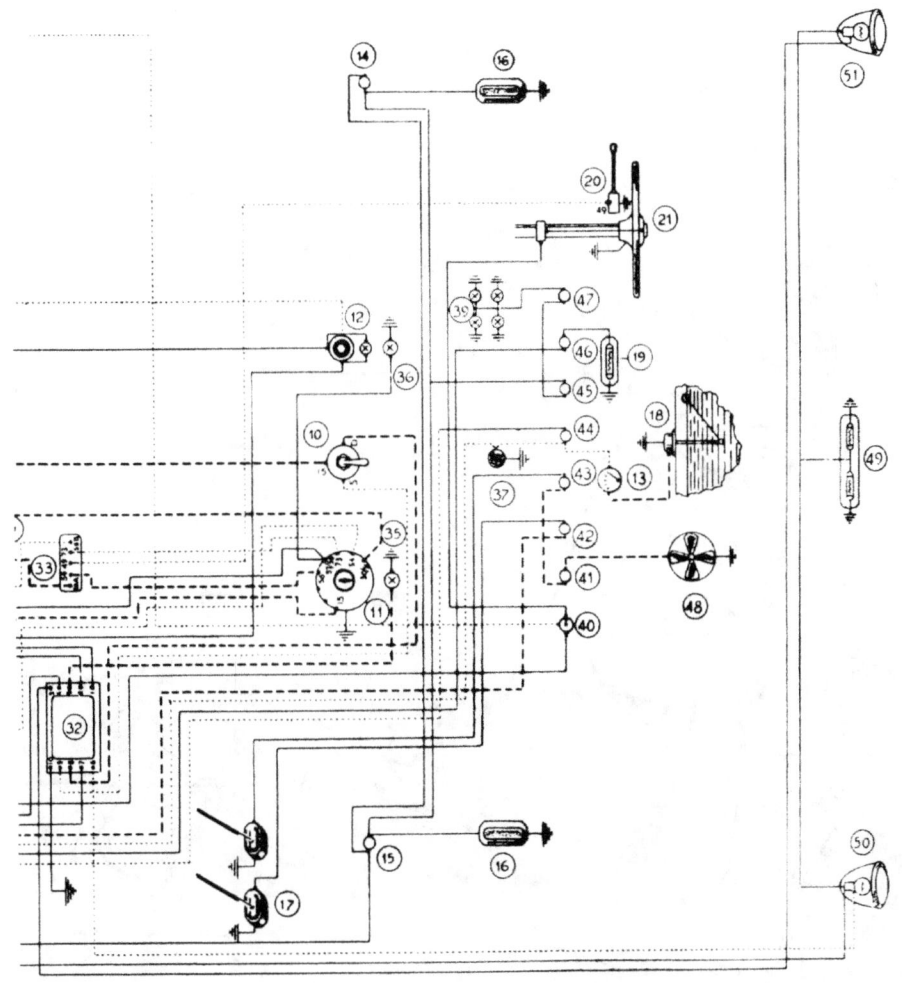

35. - Connection for indicator lamps.
36. - Head lamp dash indicator.
37. - Cigarette lighter.
38. - Additional horns.
39. - Instrument light.
40. - Horn change over switch.
41. - Temperature gauge.
42. - Left hand wiper switch.
43. - Right hand wiper switch.
44. - Fog light switch.
45. - Interior light switch.
46. - Platform light over dashboard.
47. - Platform light for dashboard.
48. - Heater.
49. - Number plate lights.
50. - Left and right trafficator lights.
51. - Left and right trafficator lights.

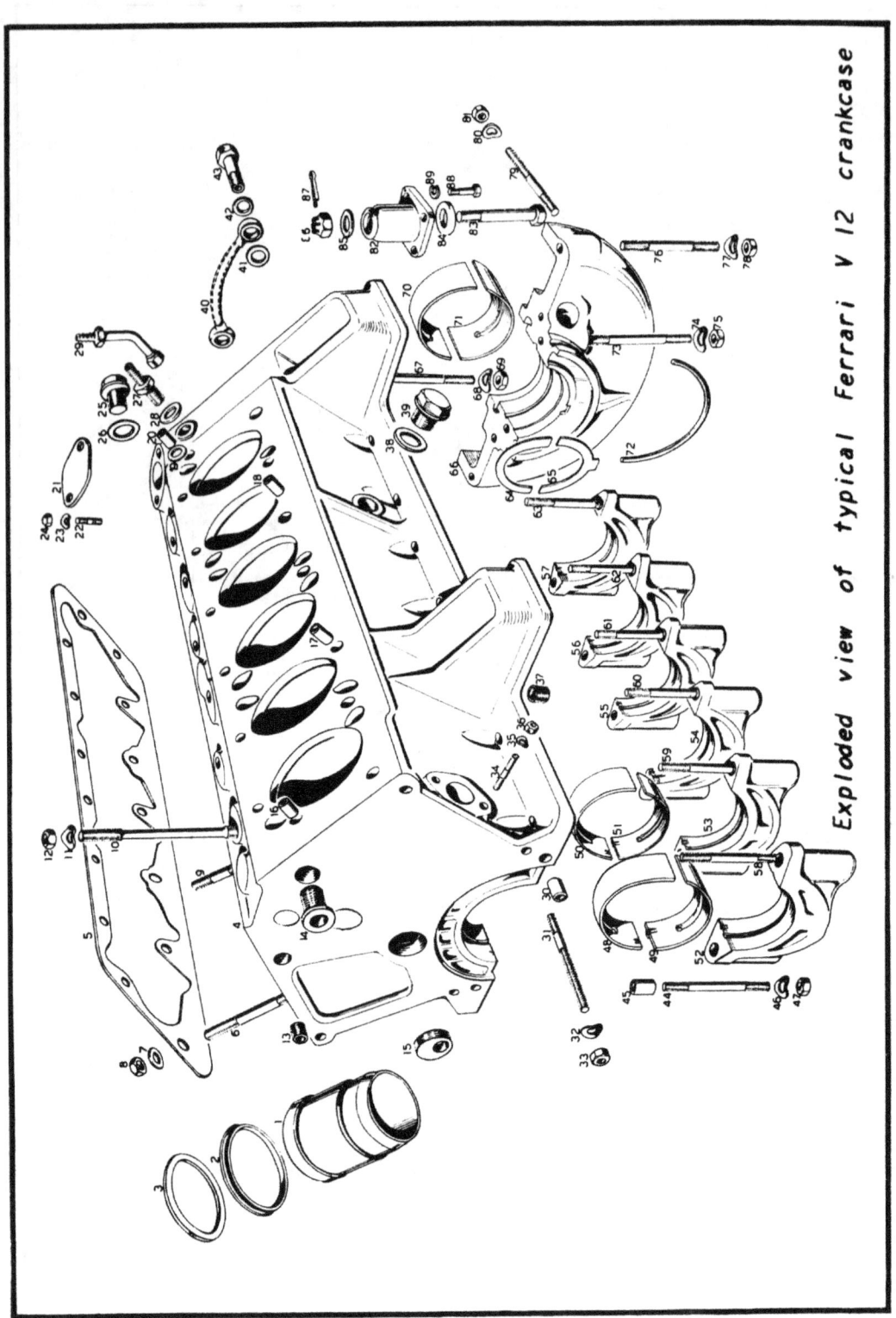

Exploded view of typical Ferrari V 12 crankcase

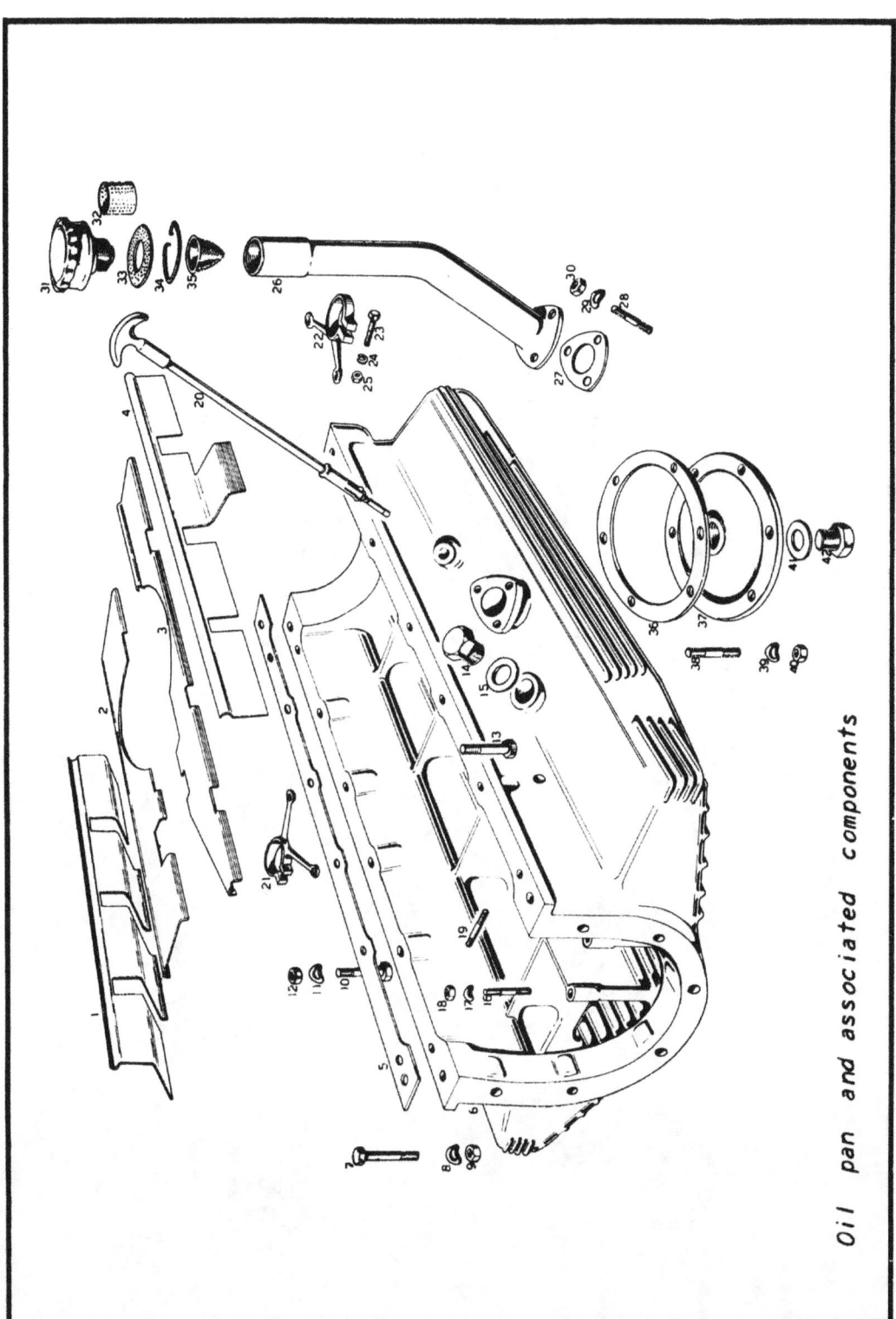

Oil pan and associated components

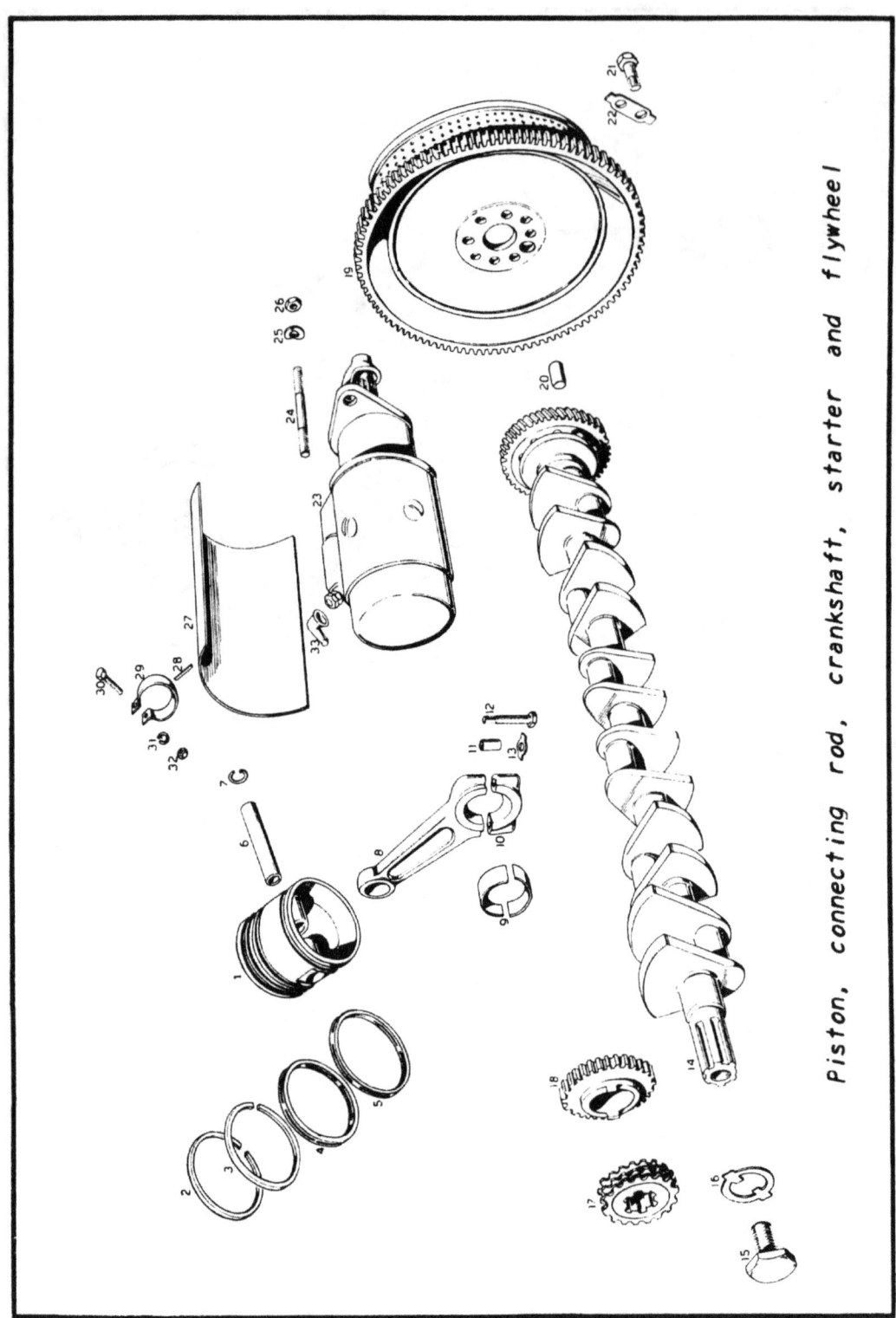

Piston, connecting rod, crankshaft, starter and flywheel

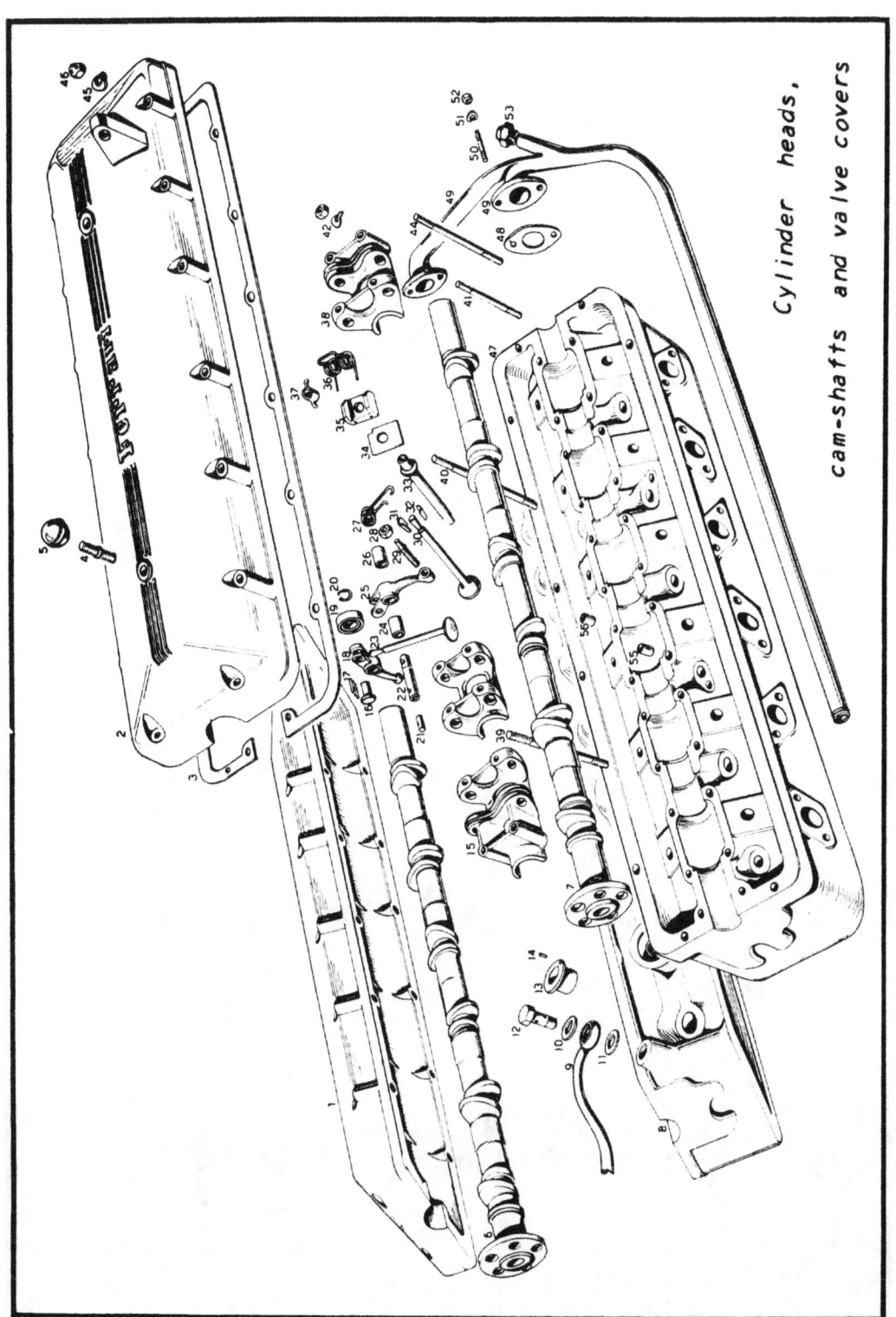

Cylinder heads, cam-shafts and valve covers

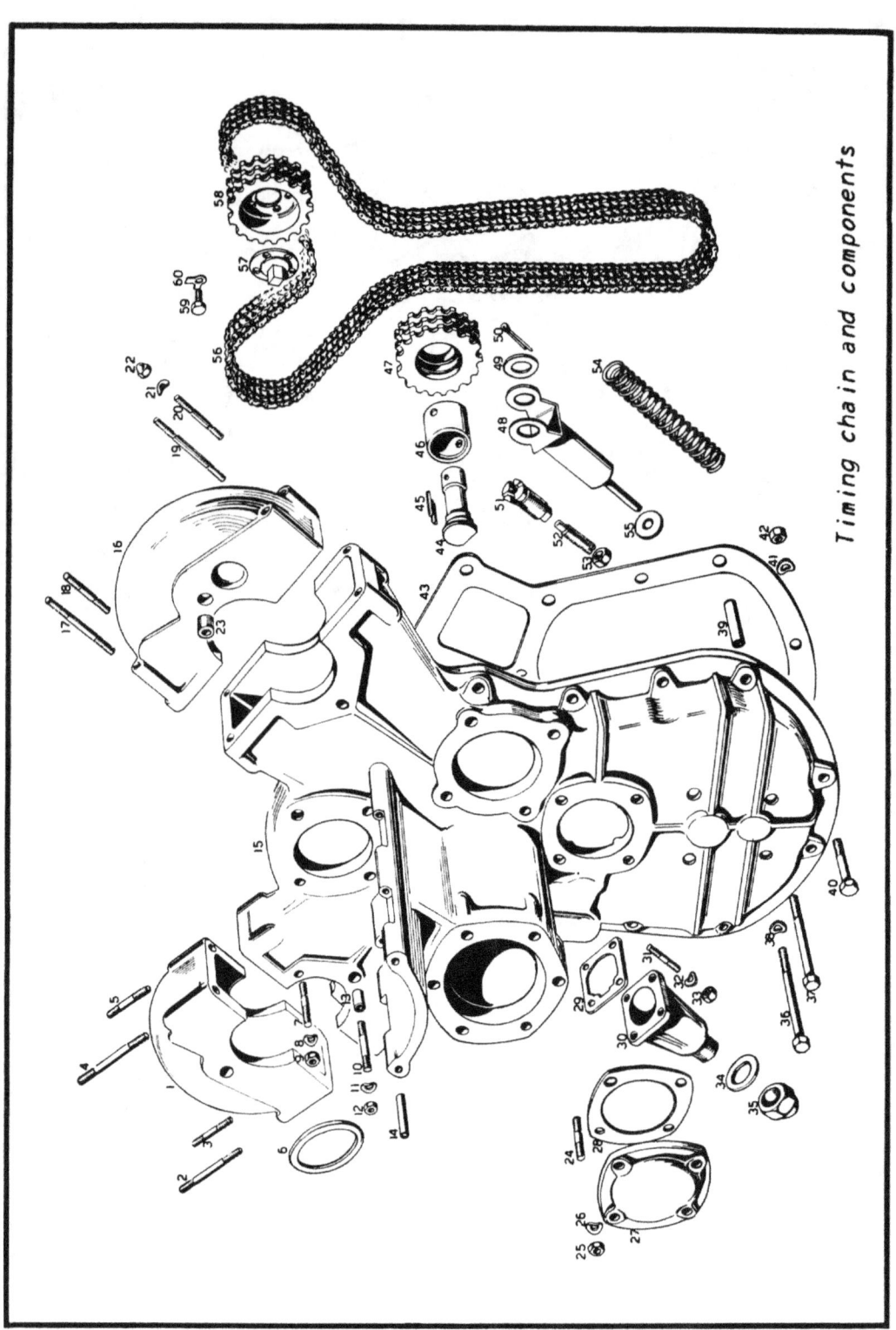

Timing chain and components

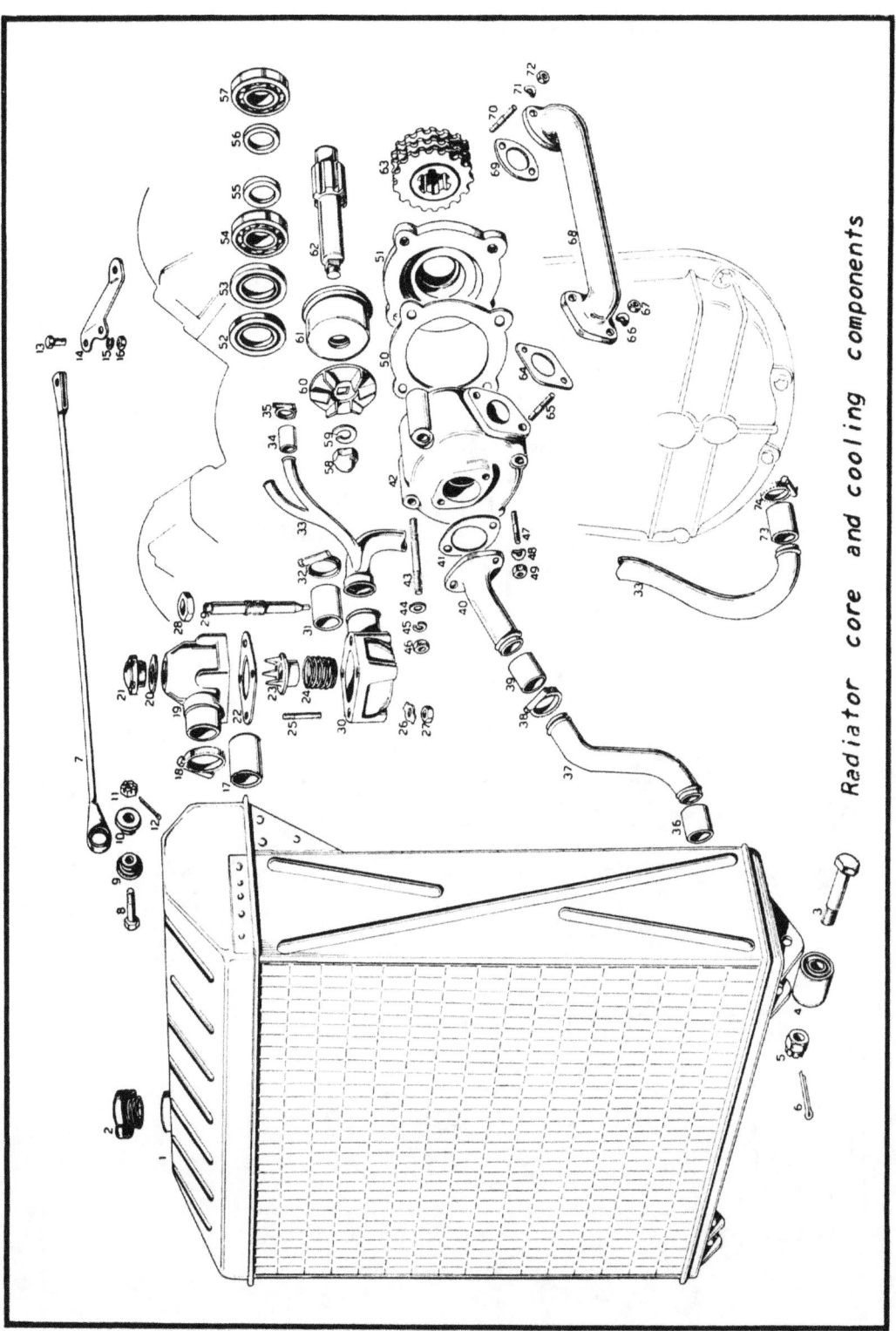

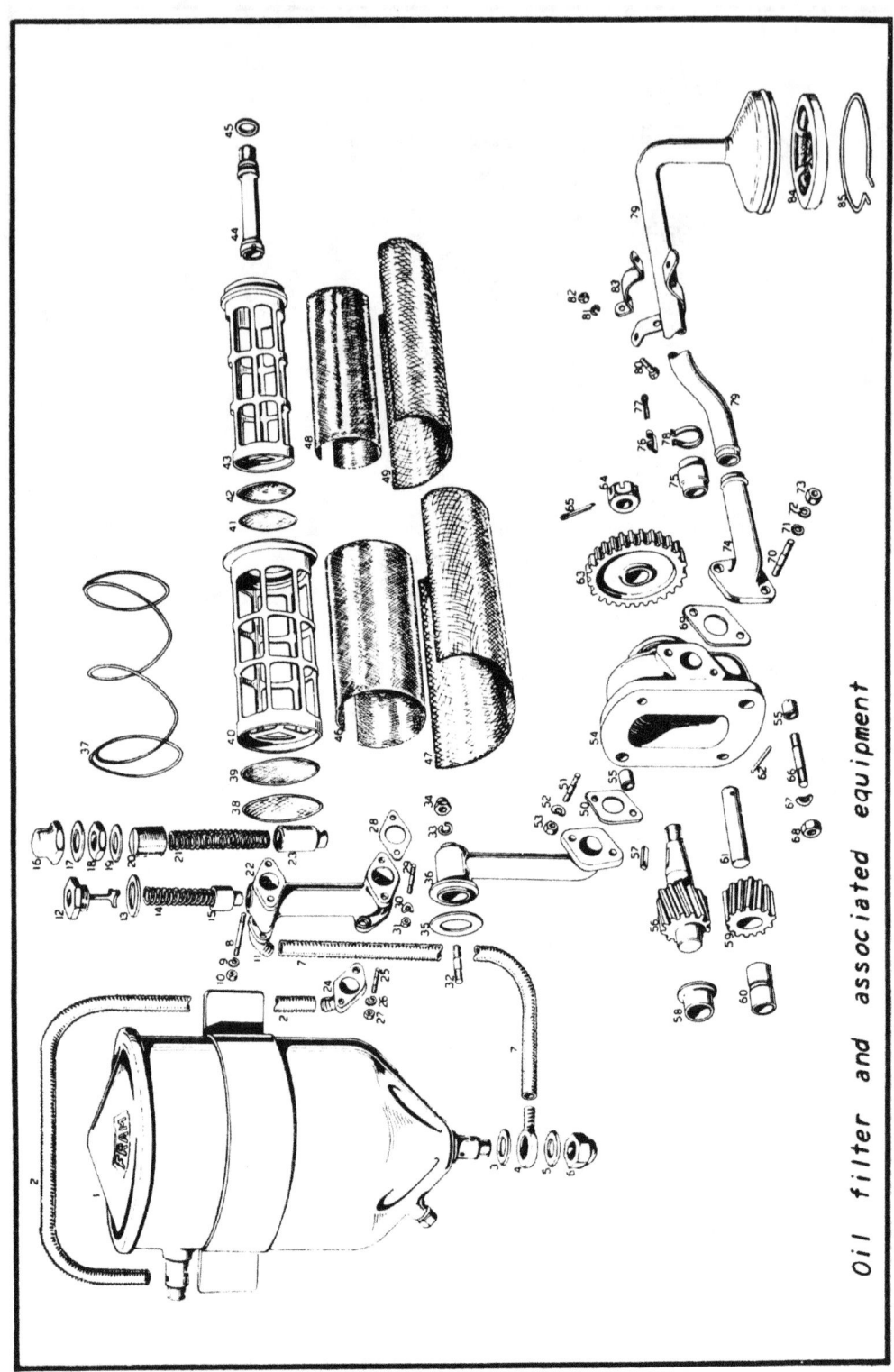

Oil filter and associated equipment

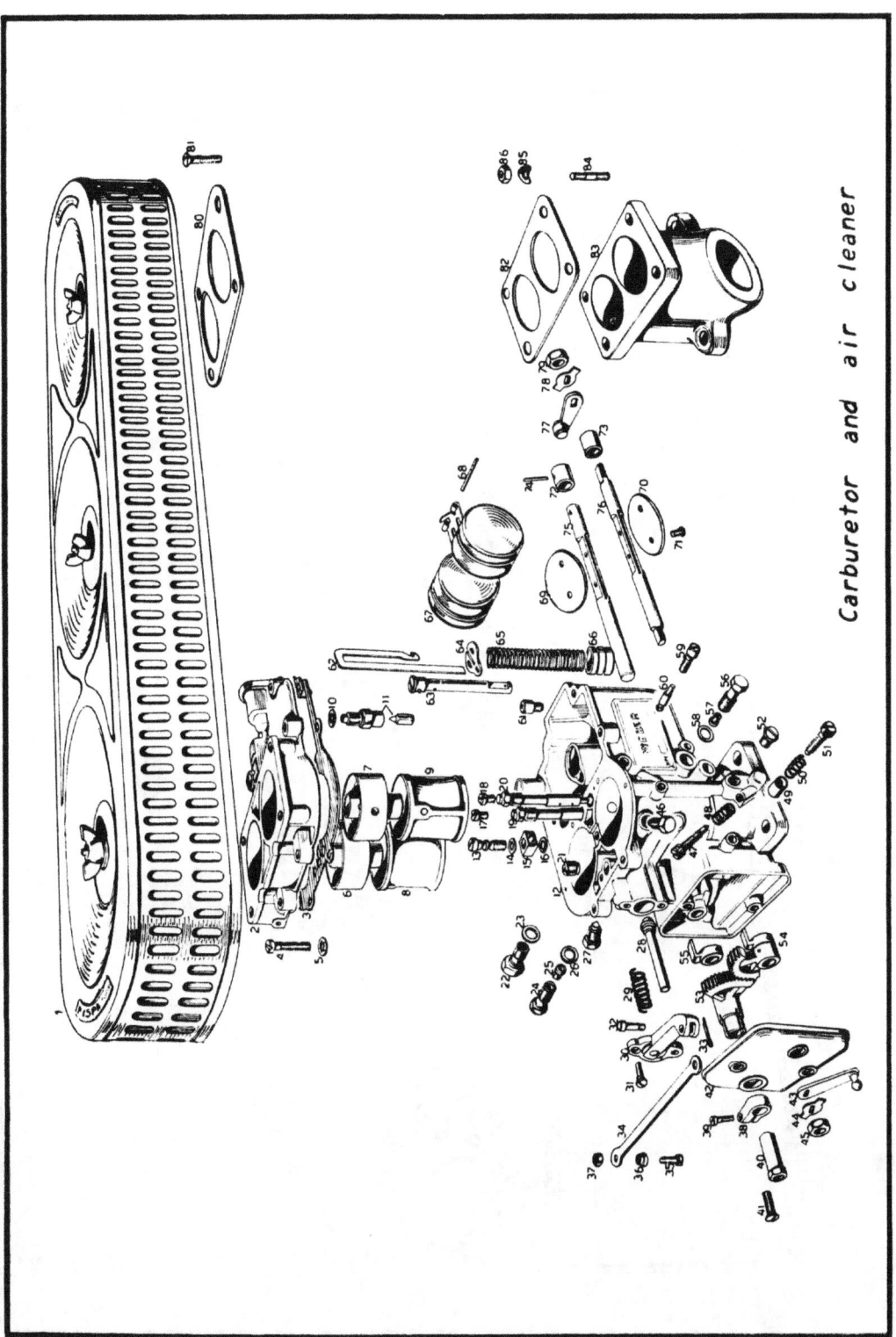

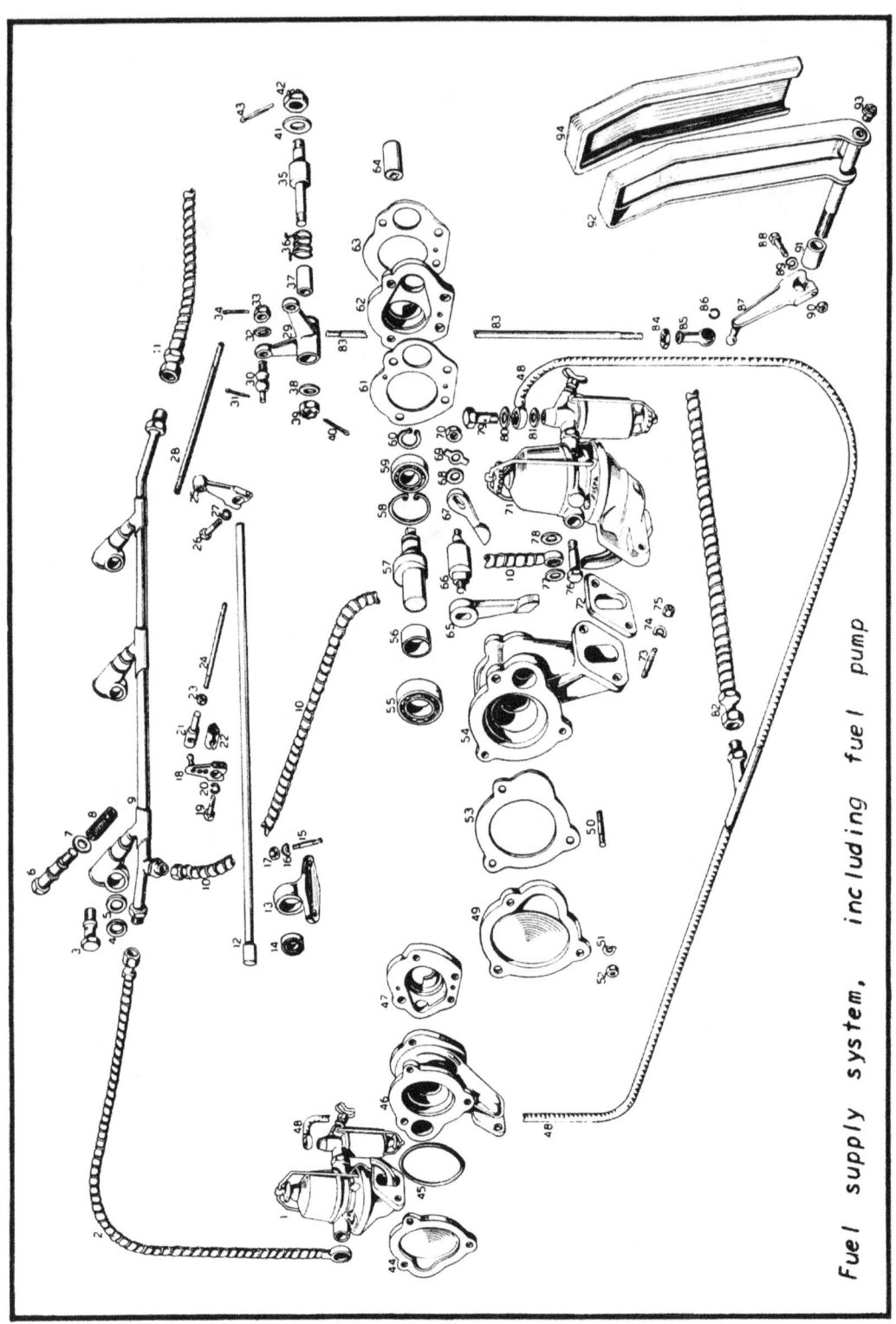

Fuel supply system, including fuel pump

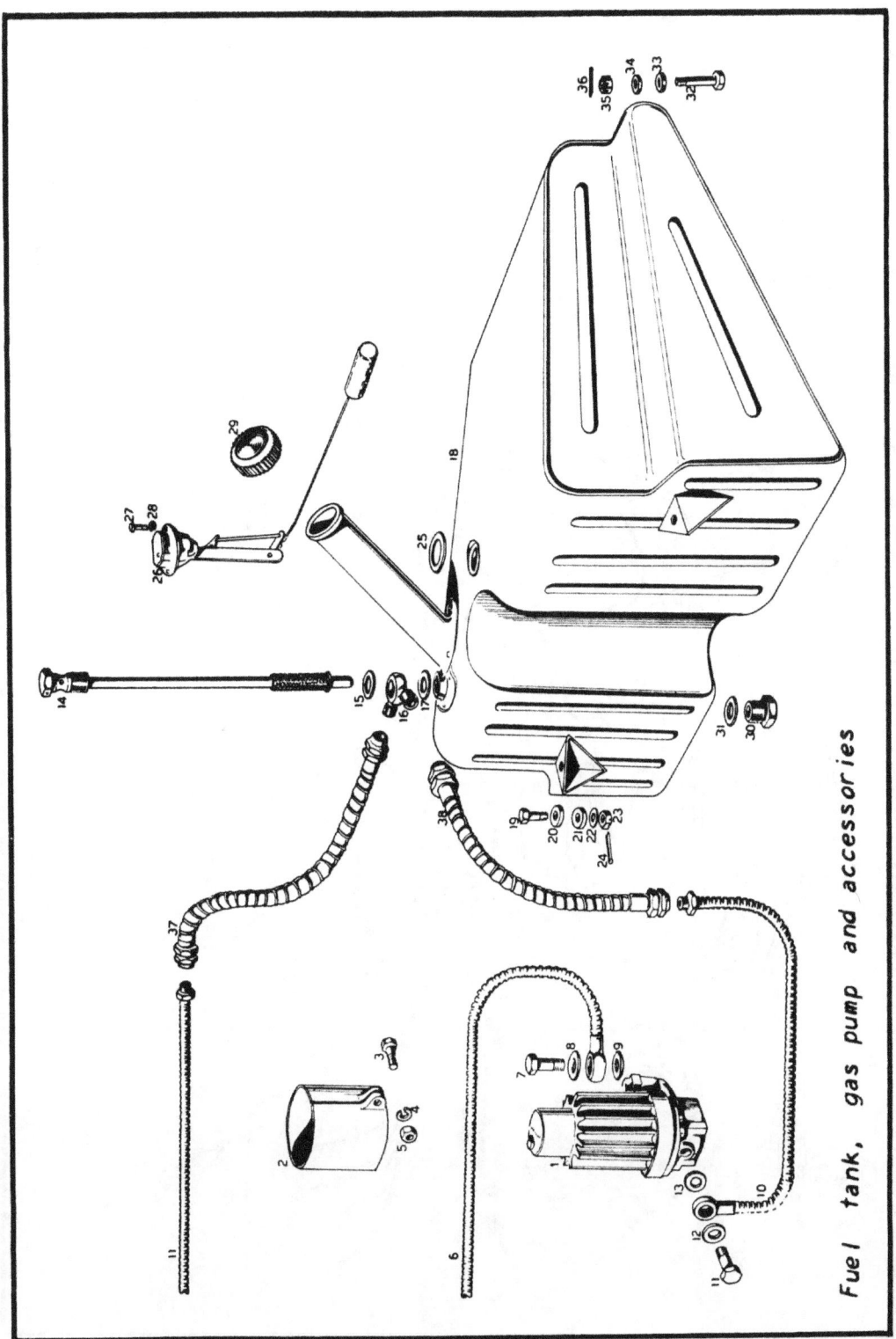

Fuel tank, gas pump and accessories

Distributor and battery

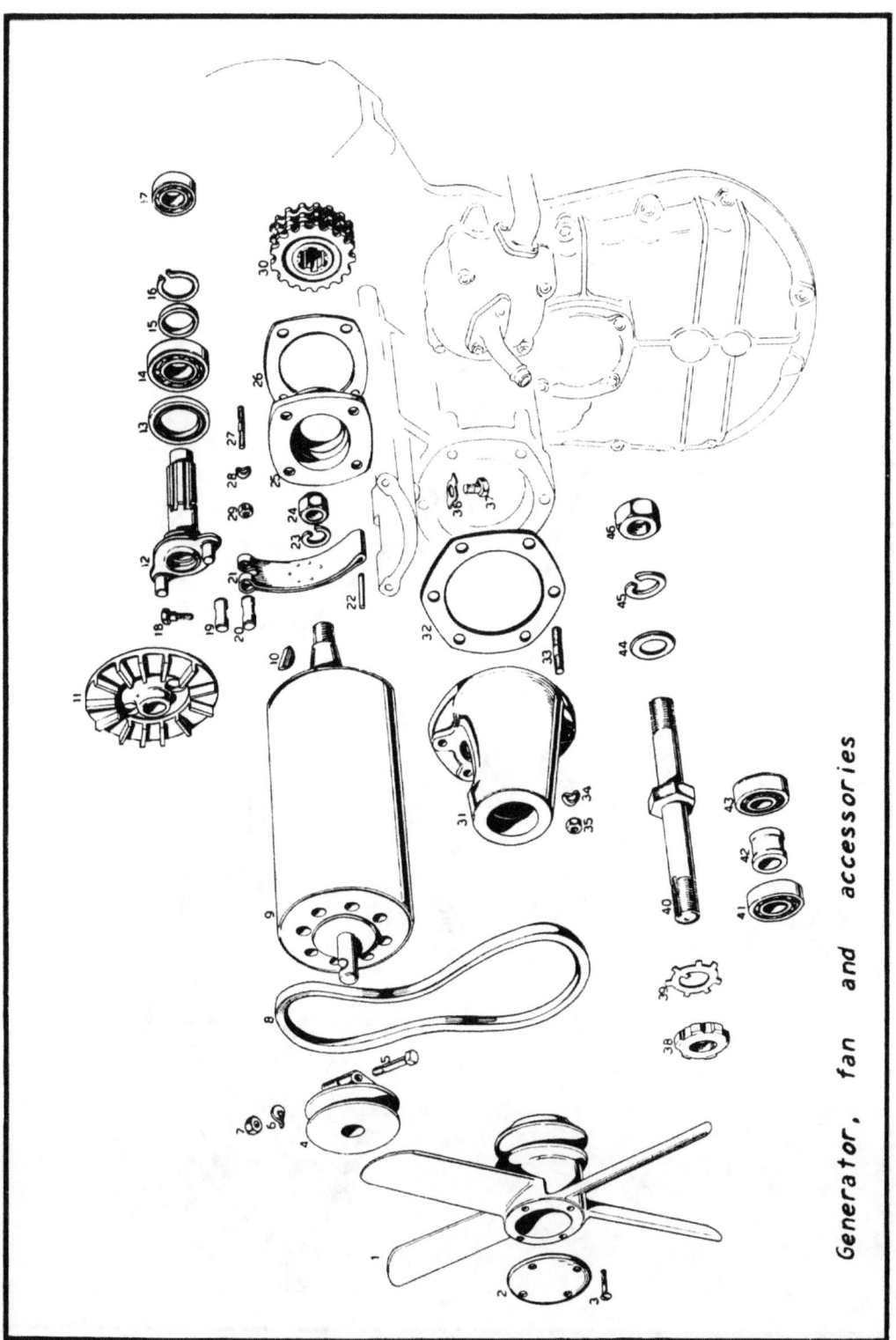

Generator, fan and accessories

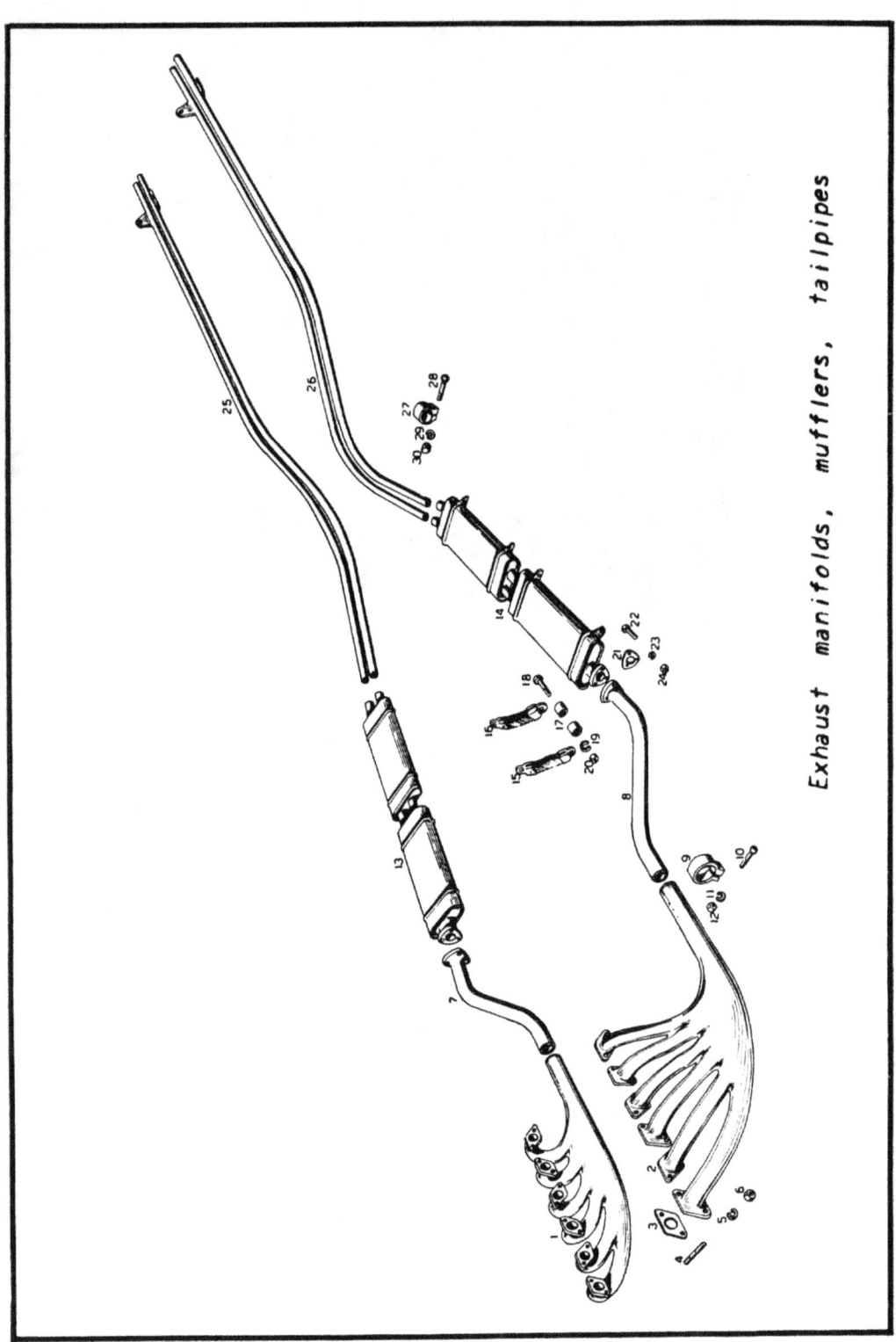

Exhaust manifolds, mufflers, tailpipes

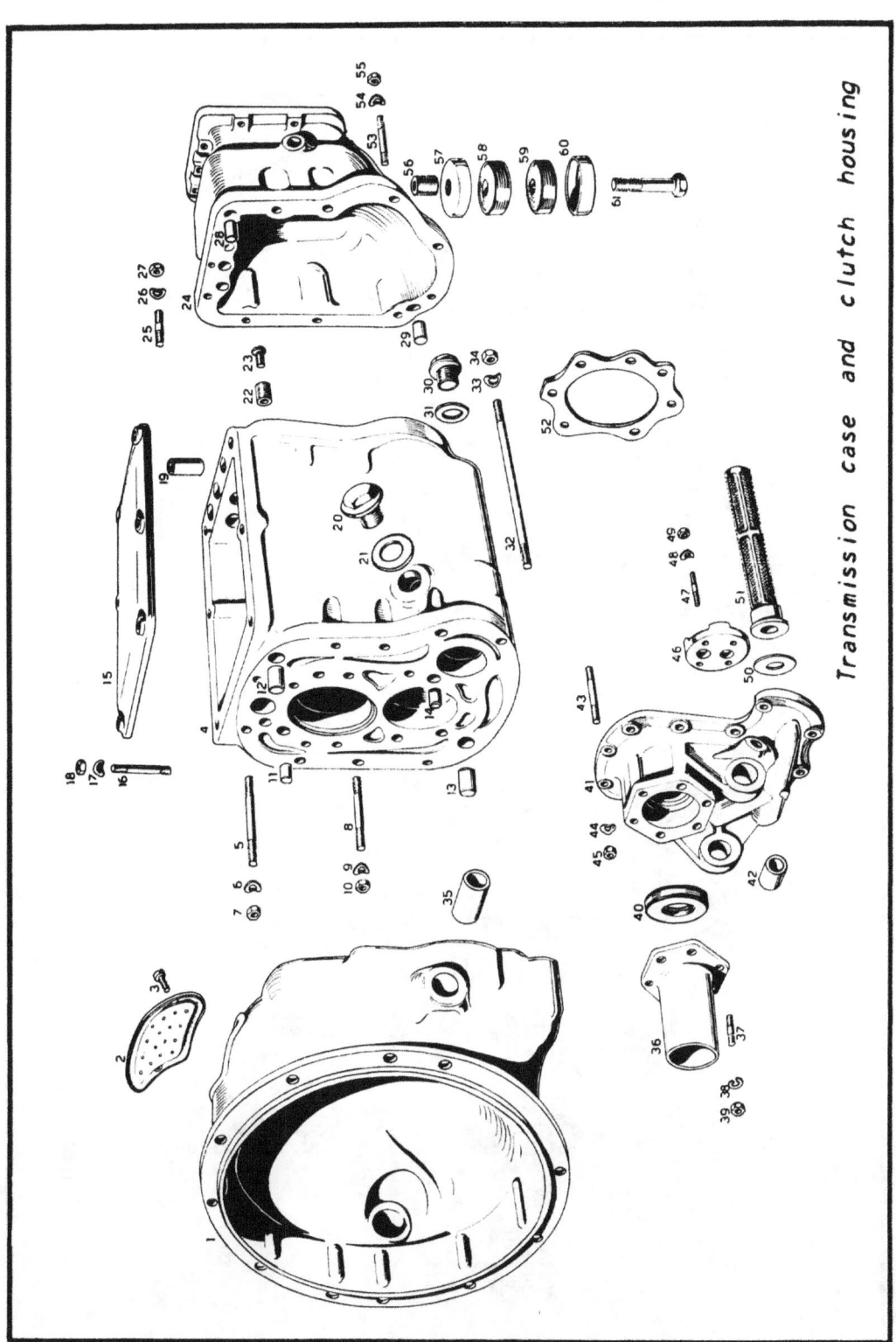

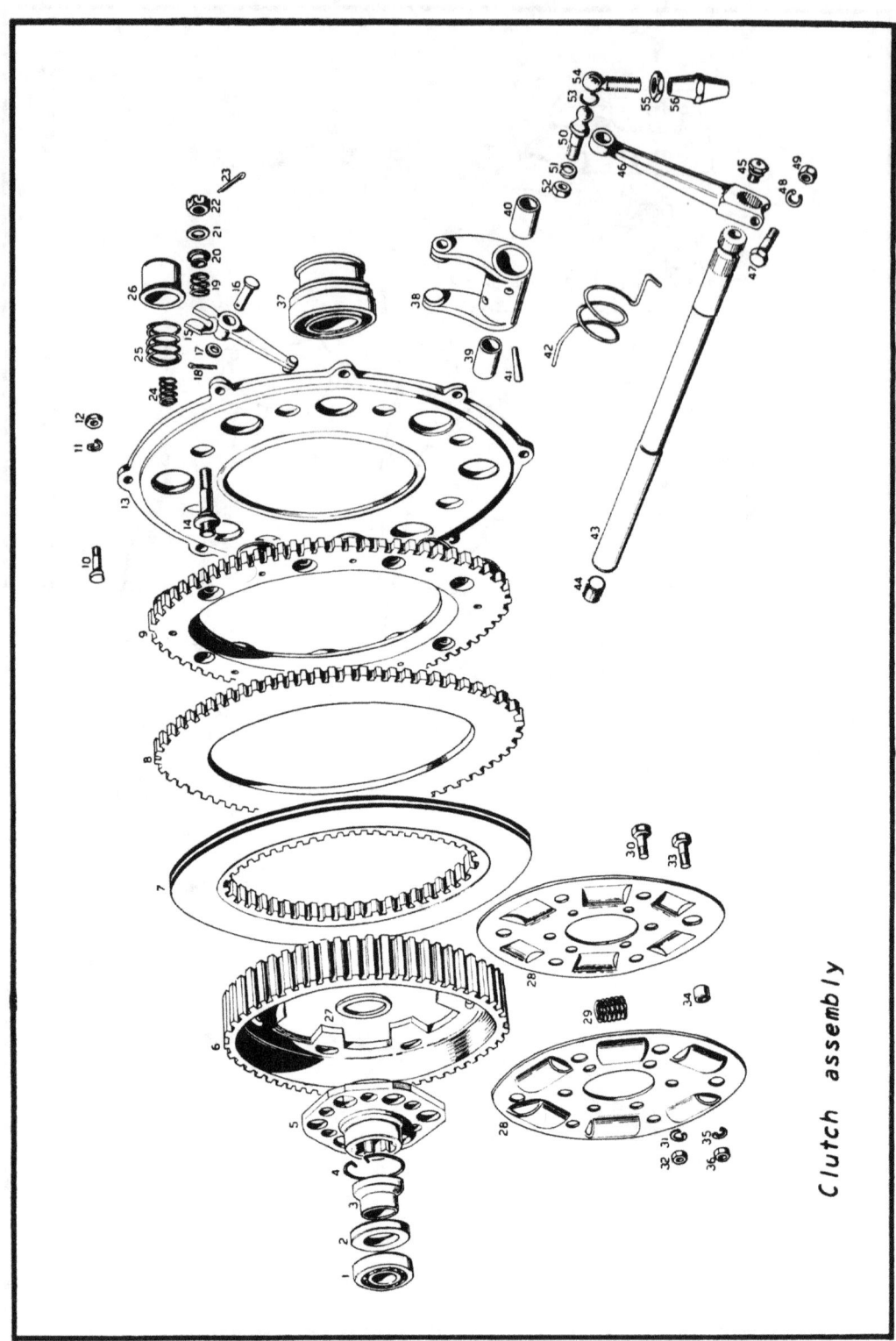

Clutch assembly

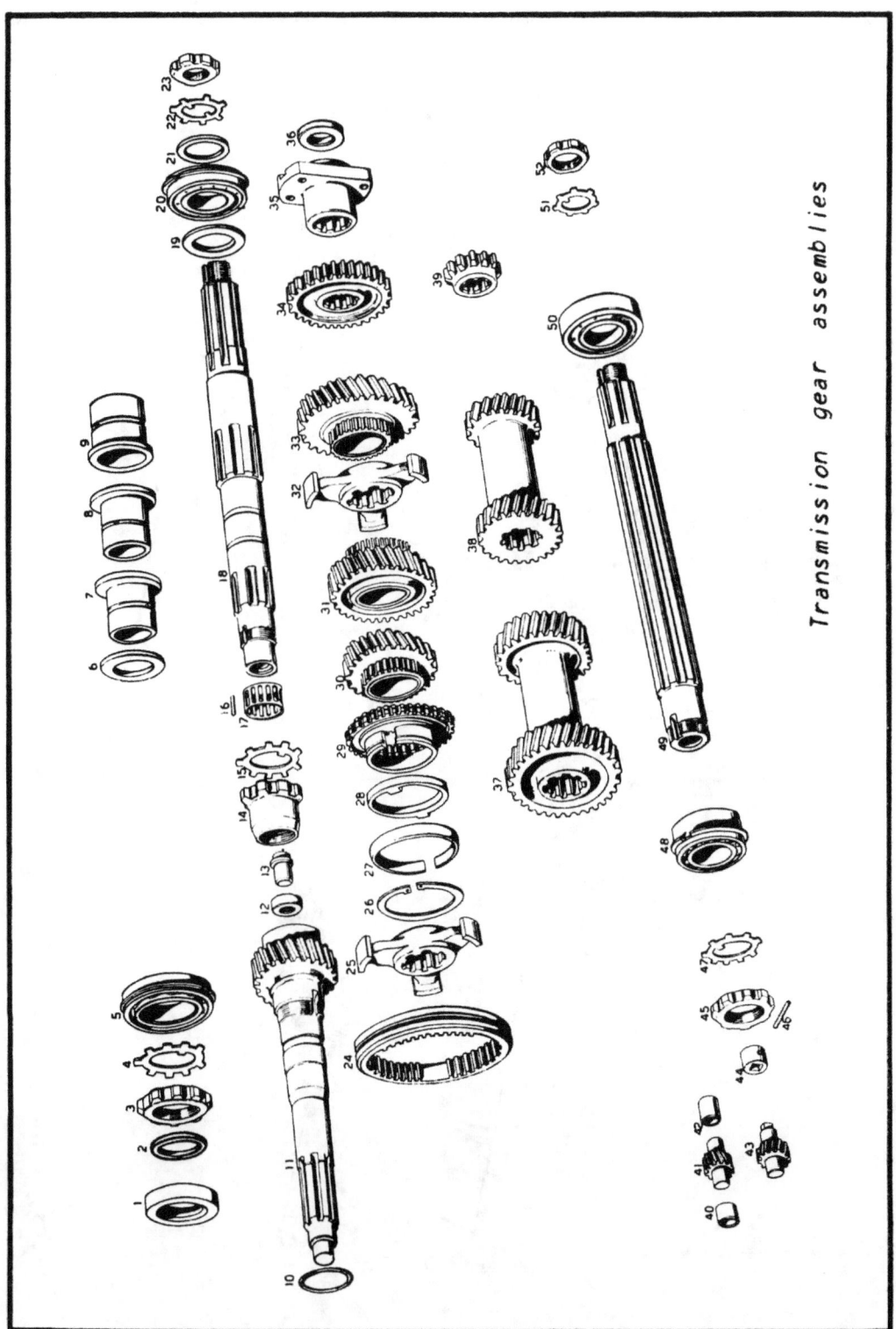

Transmission gear assemblies

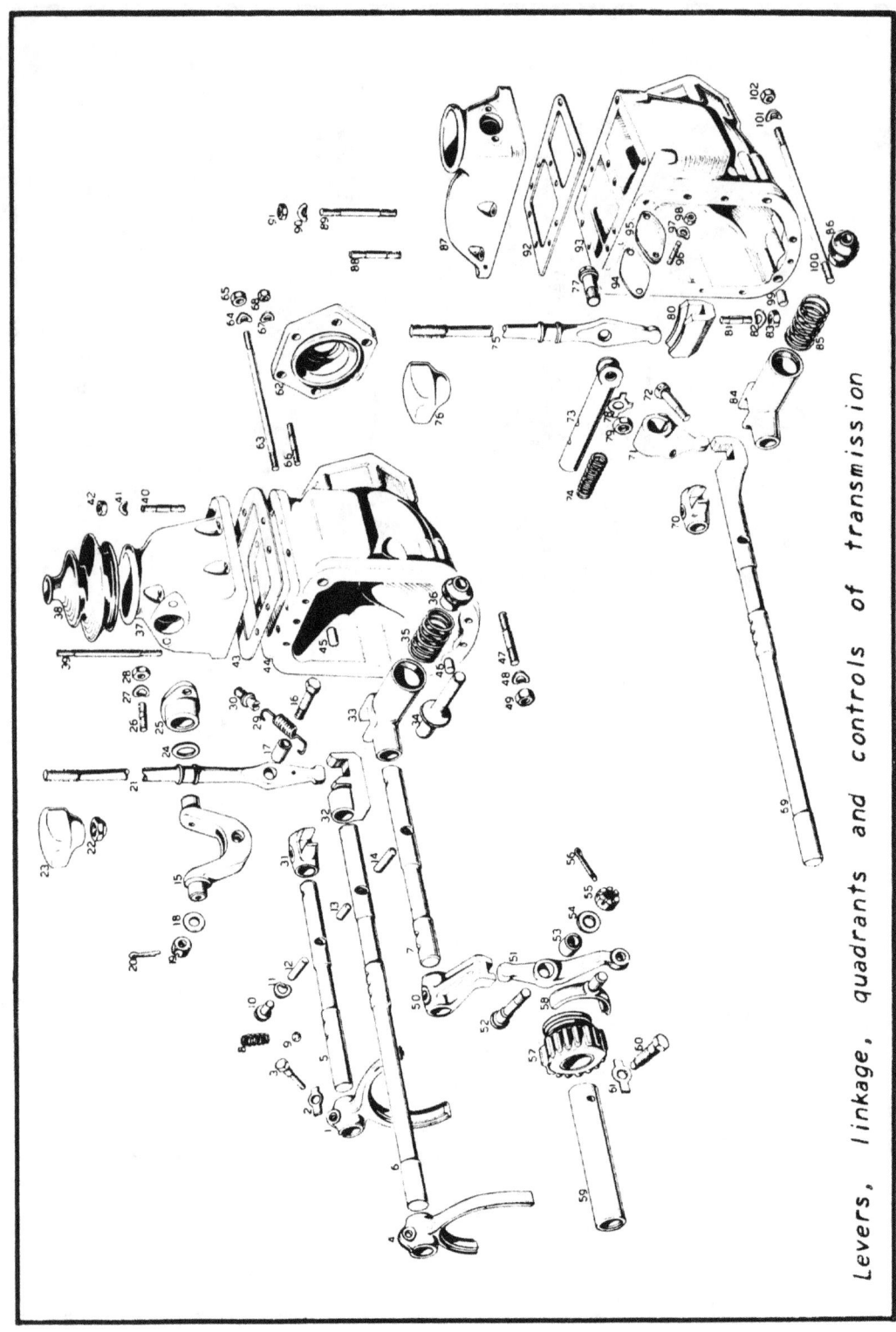

Levers, linkage, quadrants and controls of transmission

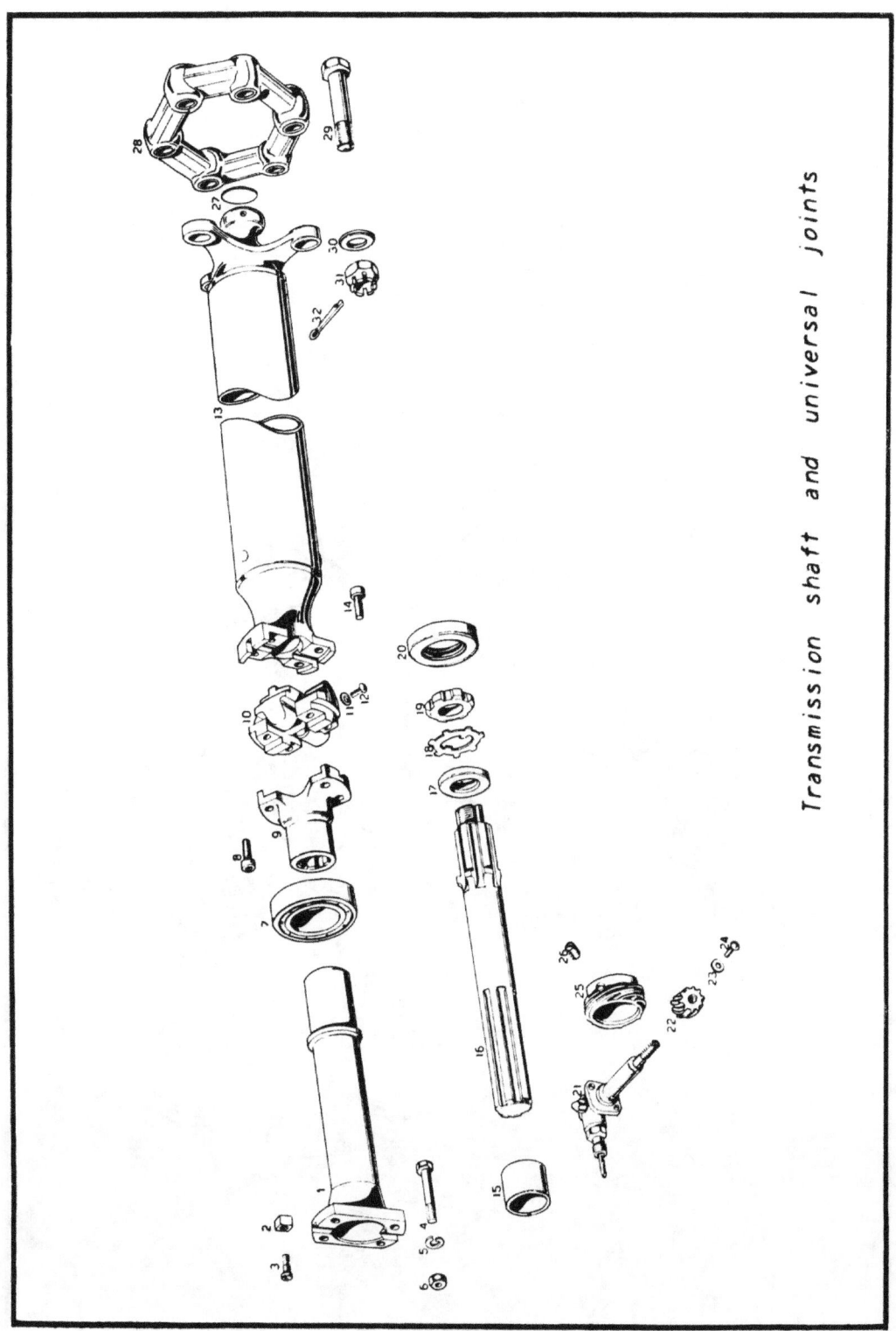
Transmission shaft and universal joints

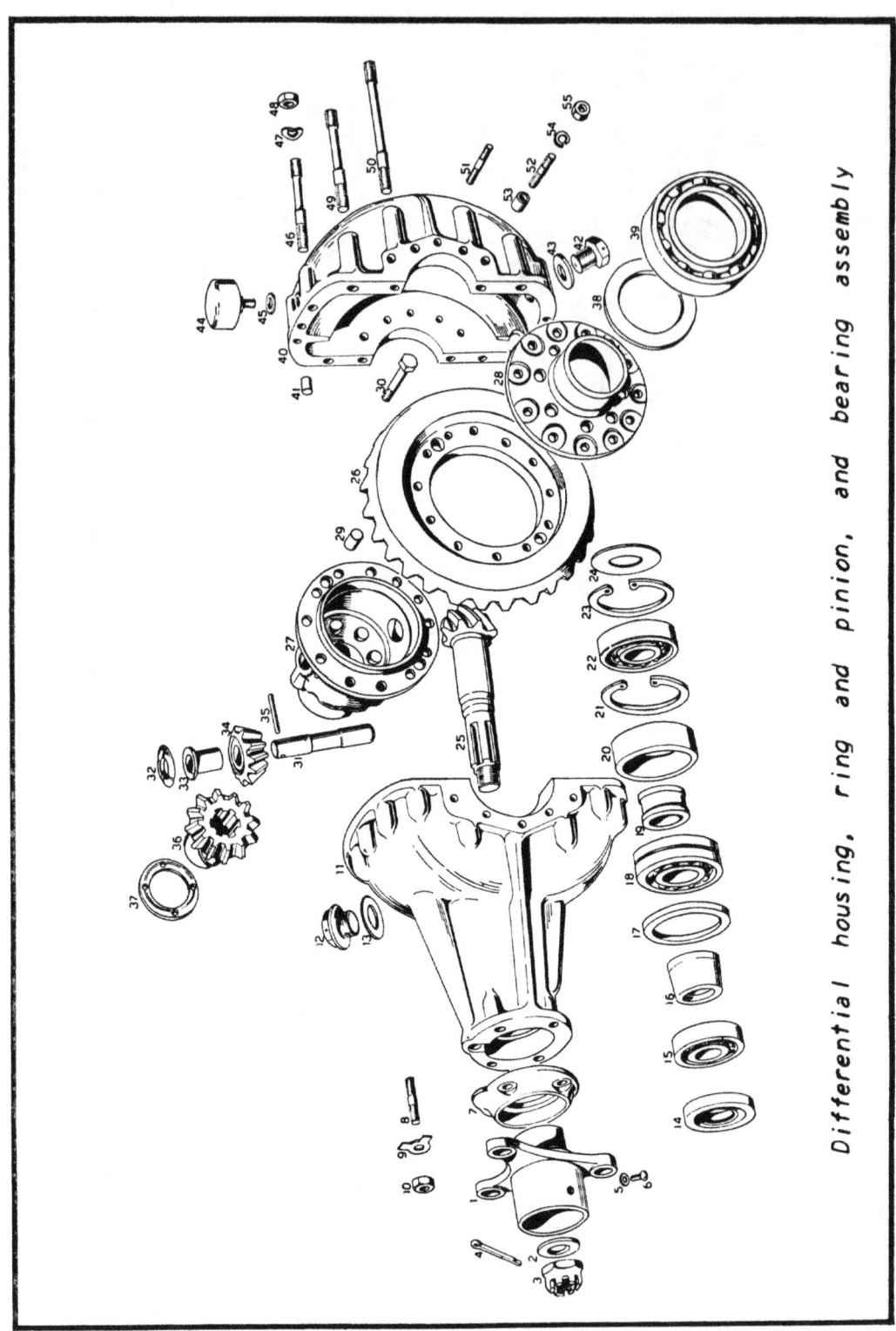

Differential housing, ring and pinion, and bearing assembly

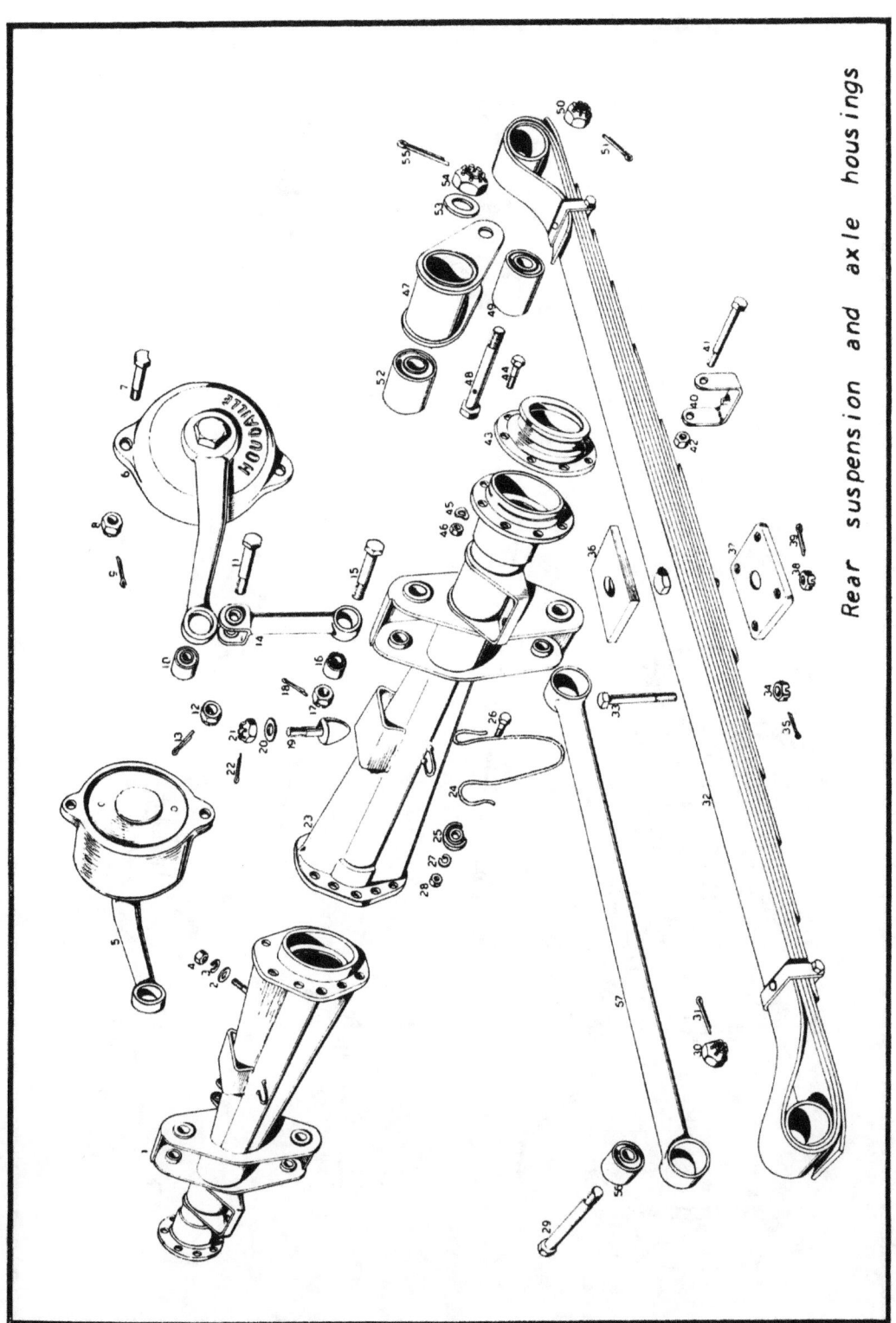

Rear suspension and axle housings

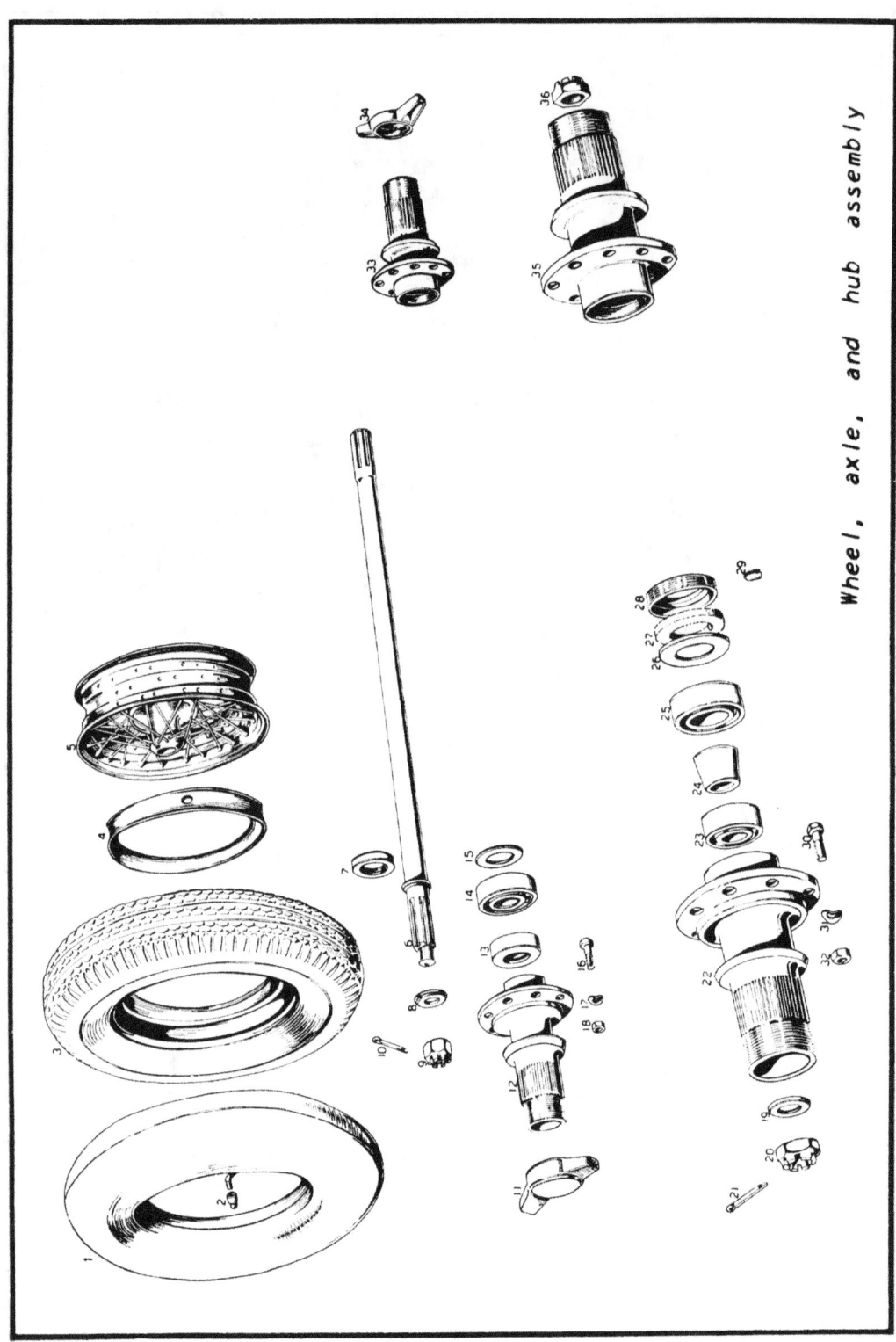

Wheel, axle, and hub assembly

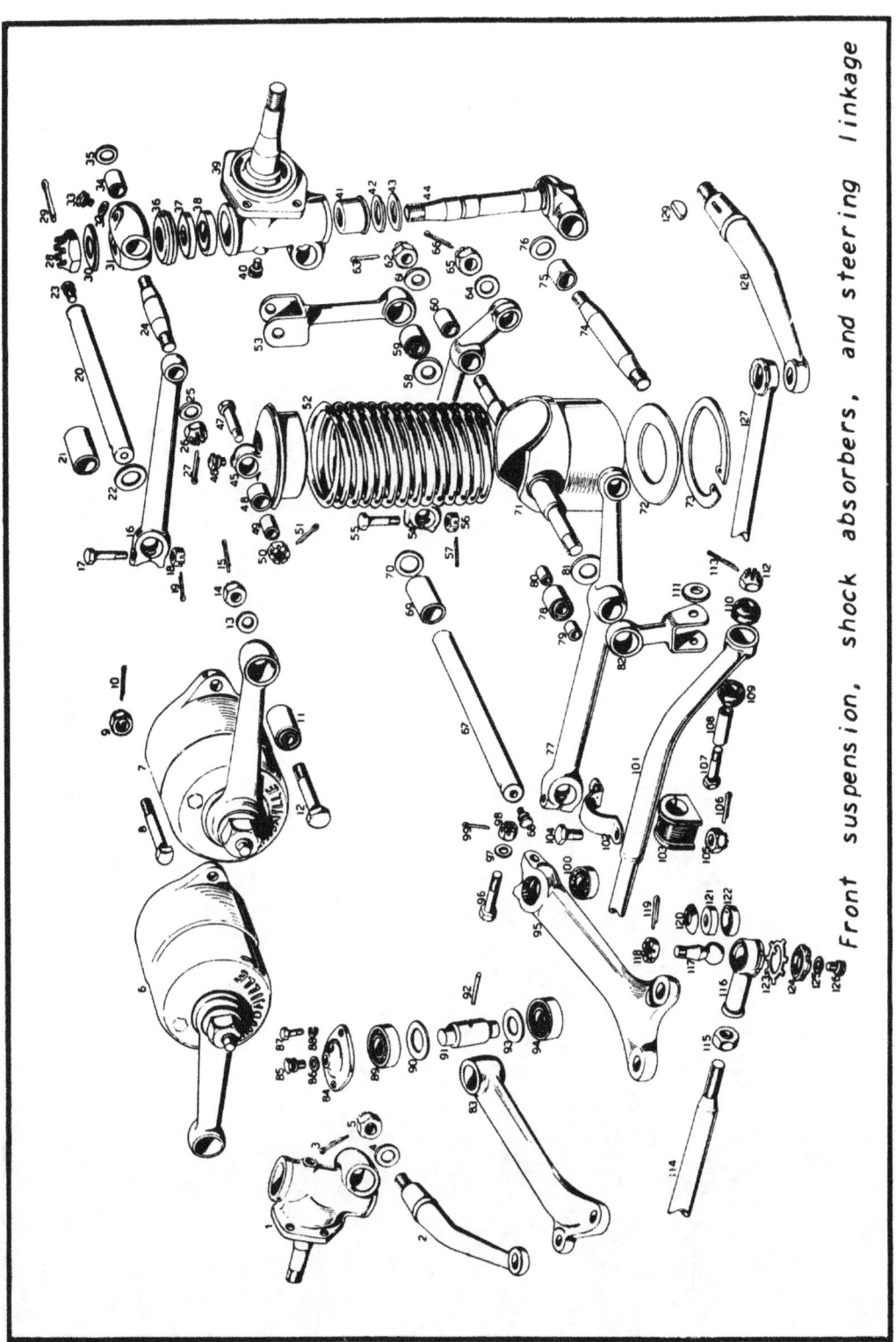

Front suspension, shock absorbers, and steering linkage

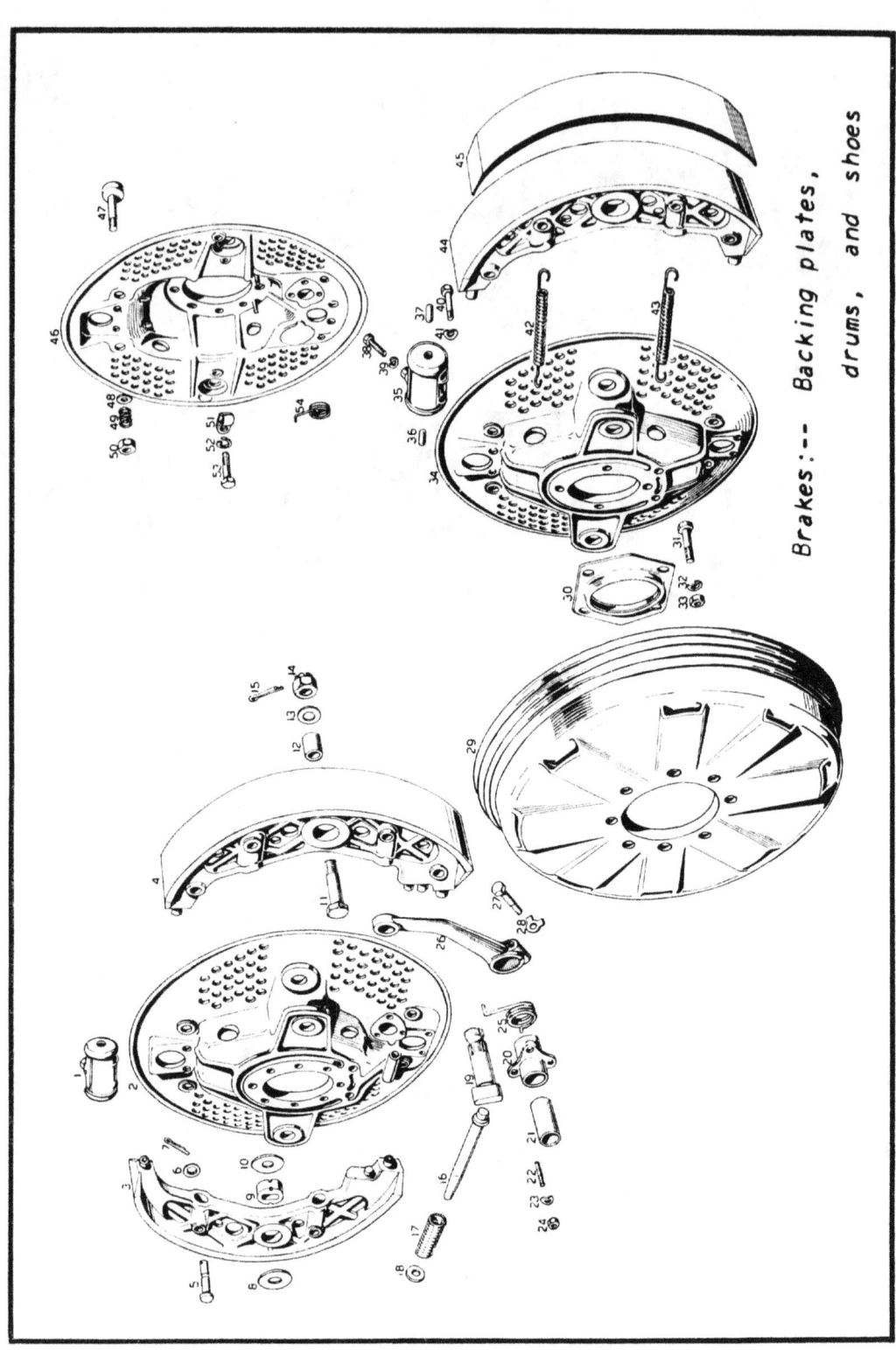

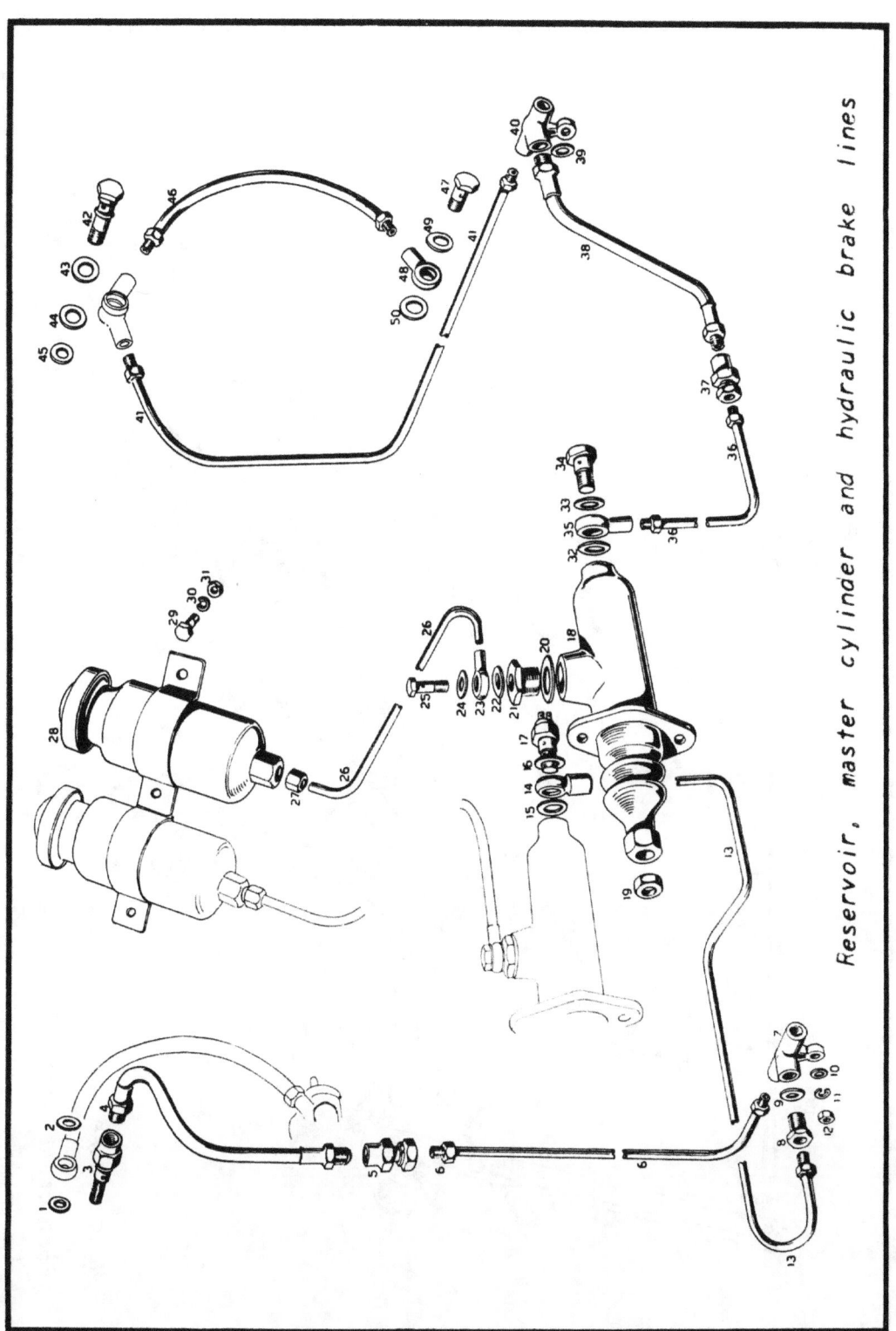

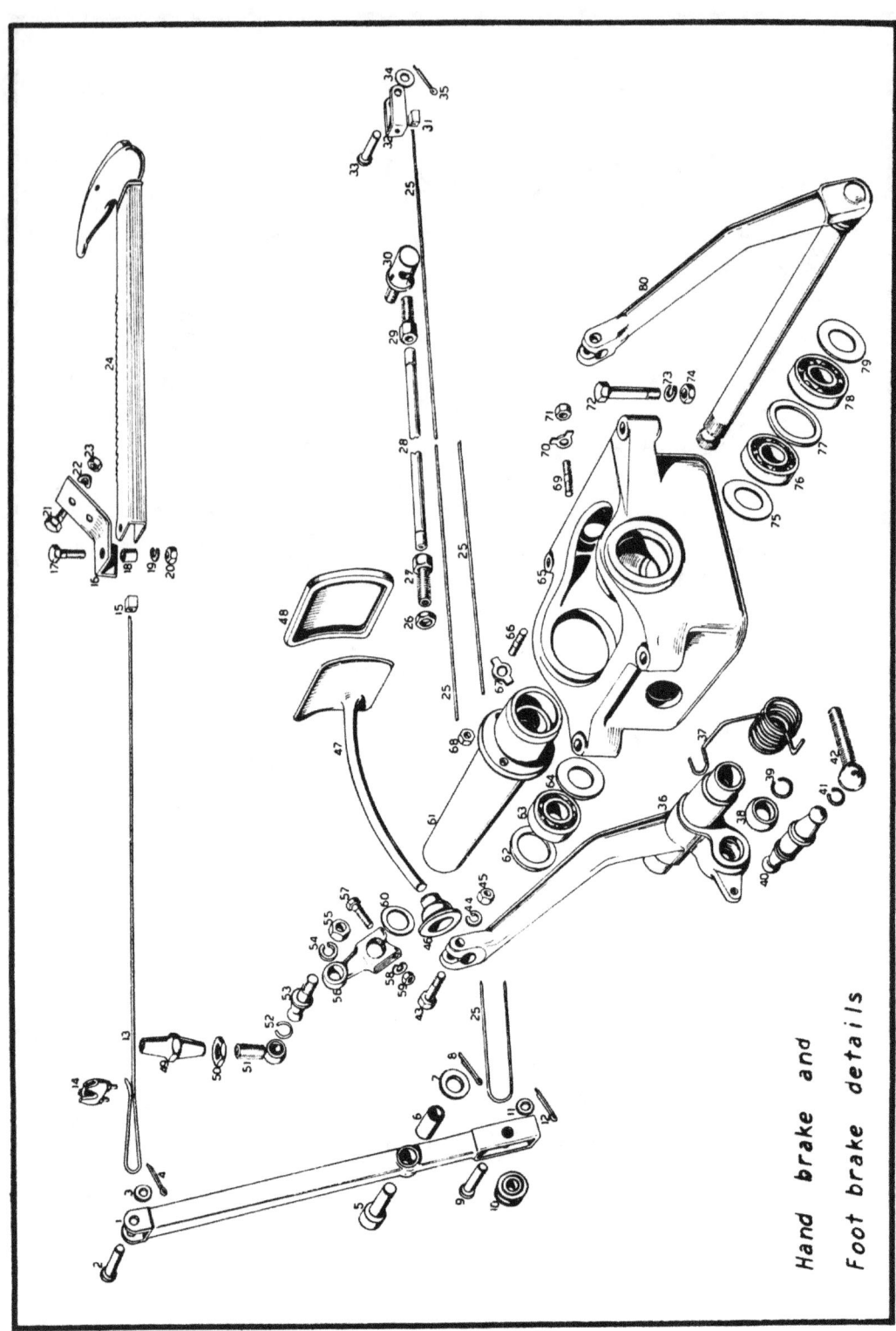

Hand brake and Foot brake details

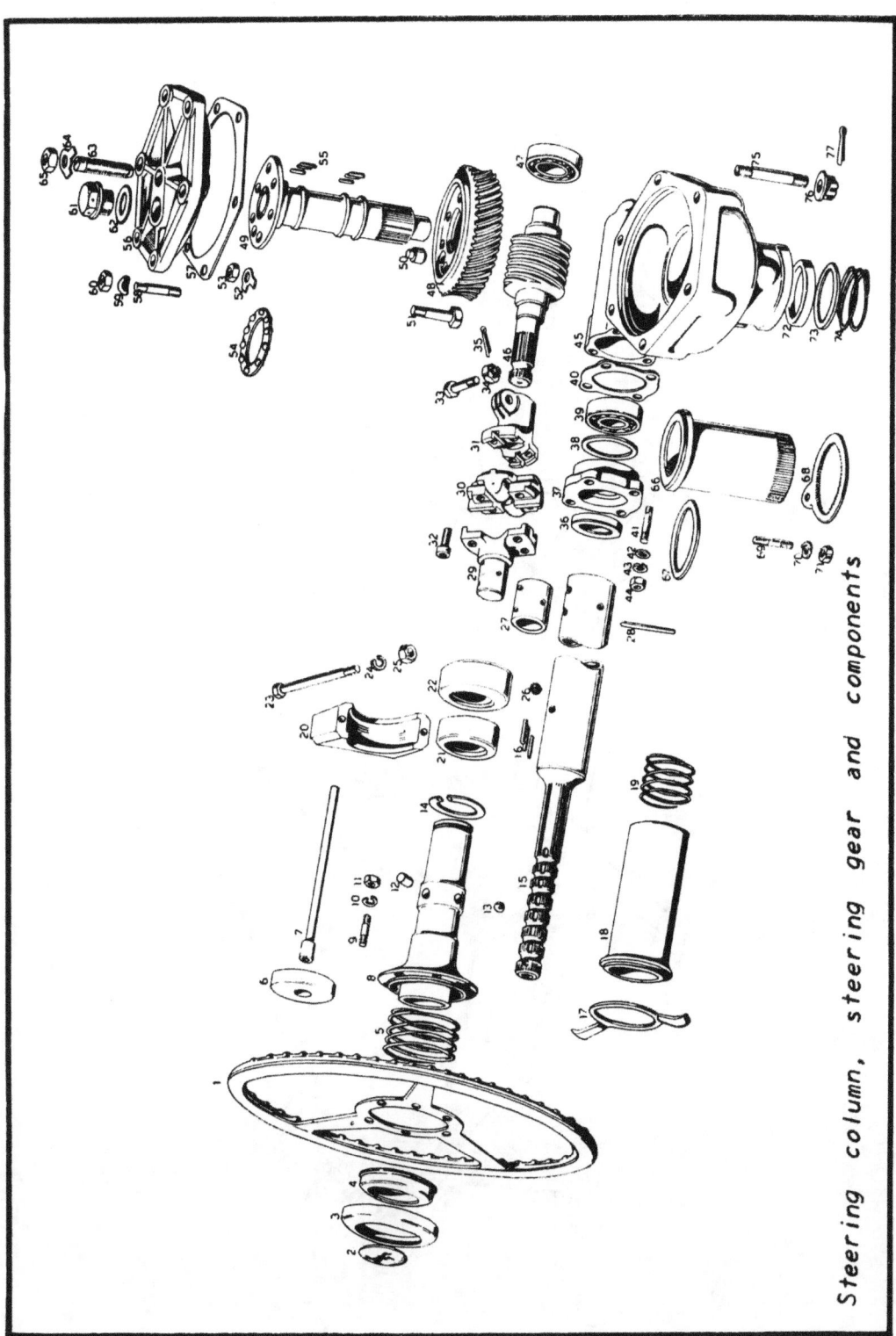

Steering column, steering gear and components

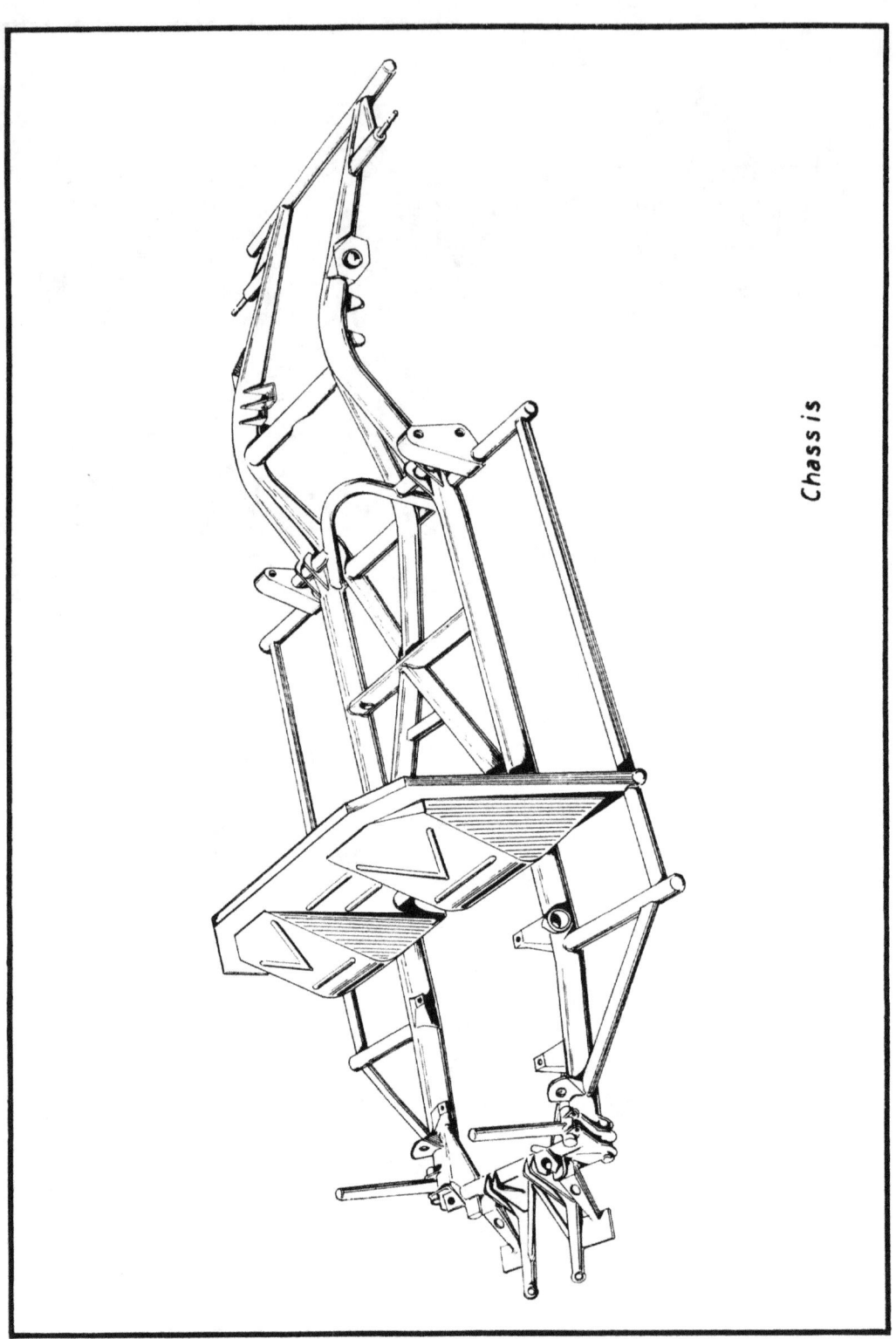

Chassis

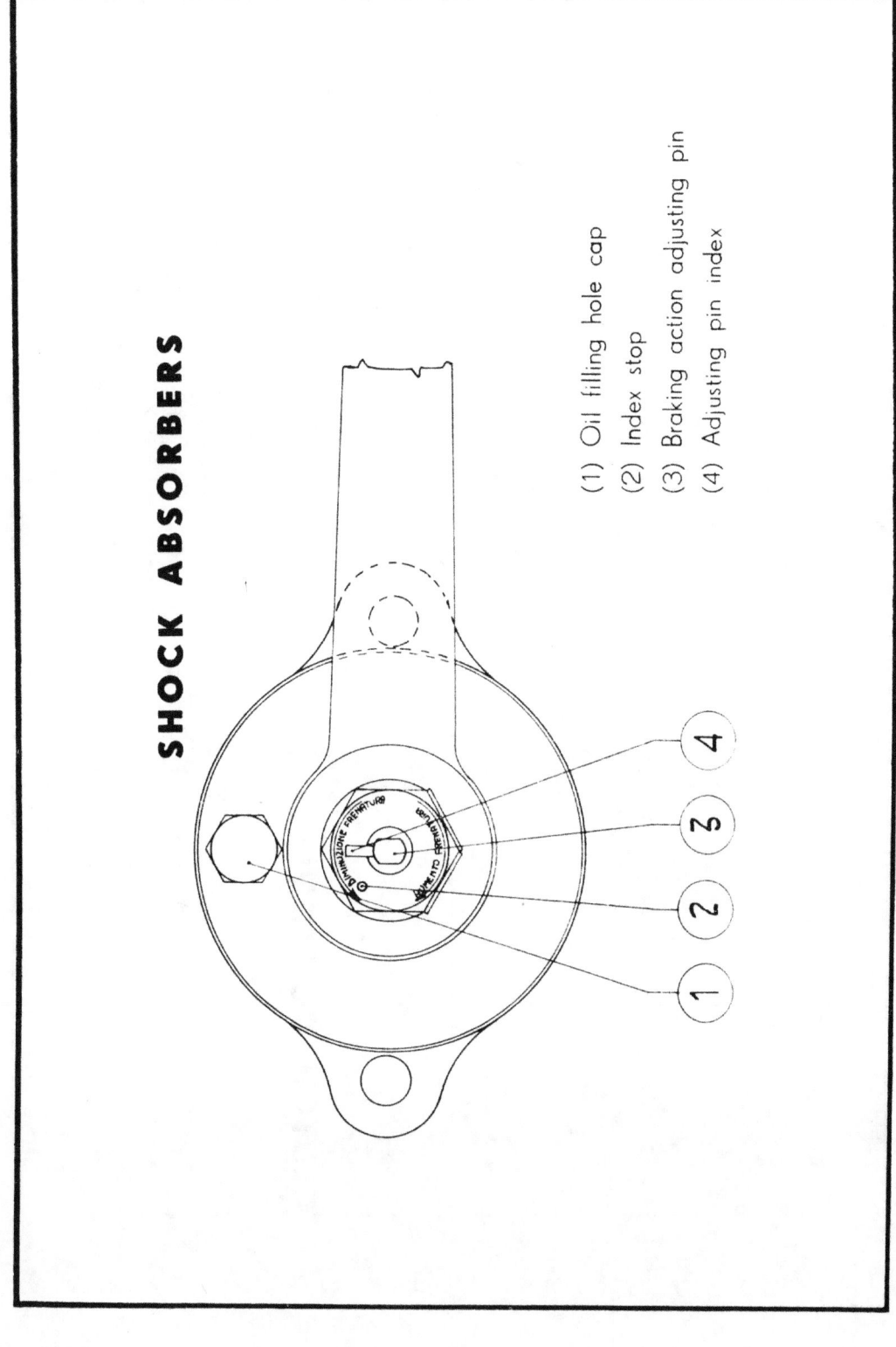

SHOCK ABSORBERS

(1) Oil filling hole cap
(2) Index stop
(3) Braking action adjusting pin
(4) Adjusting pin index

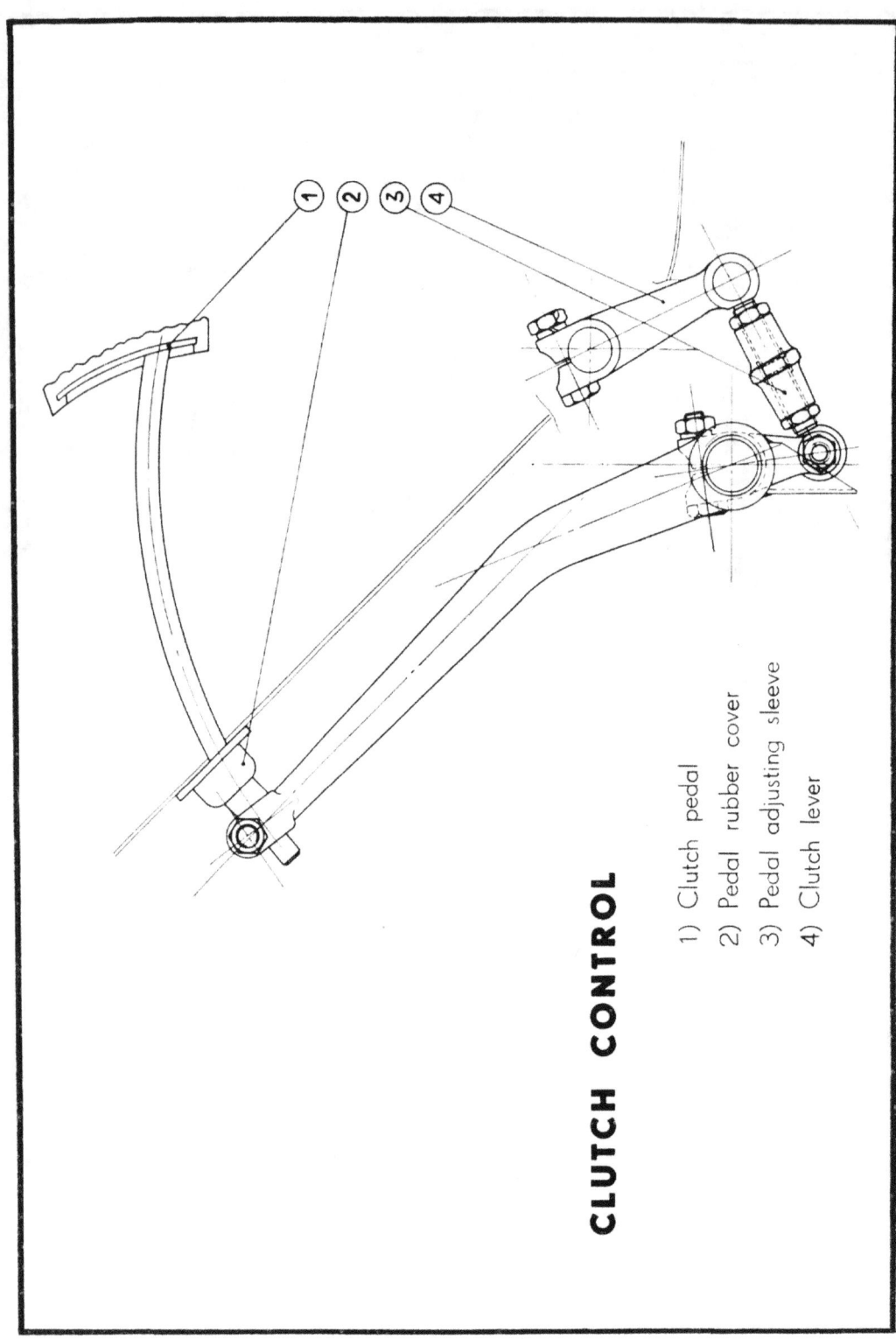

CLUTCH CONTROL

1) Clutch pedal
2) Pedal rubber cover
3) Pedal adjusting sleeve
4) Clutch lever

CLUTCH ADJUSTMENT DIAGRAM.

1. Brake pedal.
2. Pedal return spring.
3. Adjustment lock nut.
4. Brake adjustment nut.
5. Connection to brake arrangement

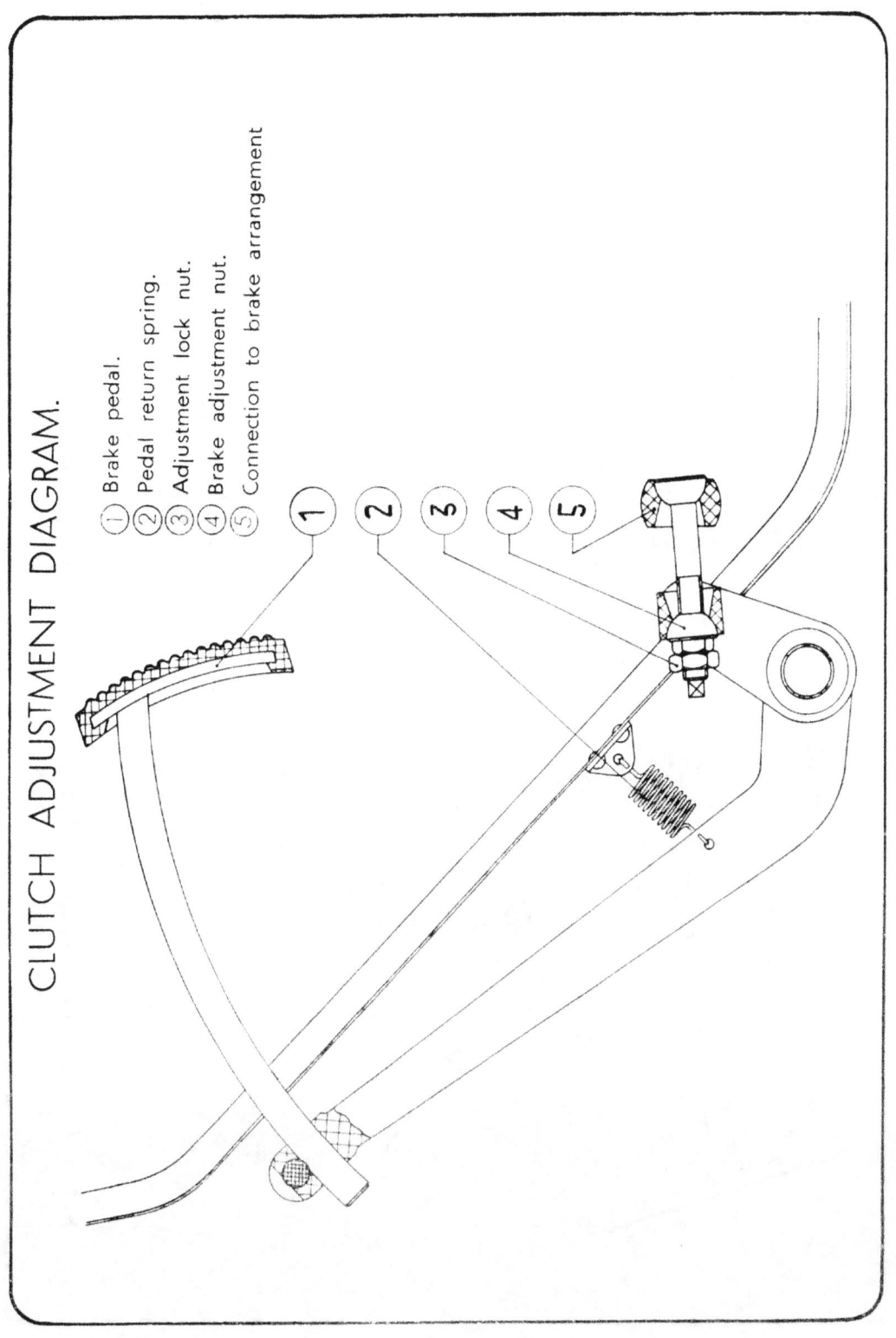

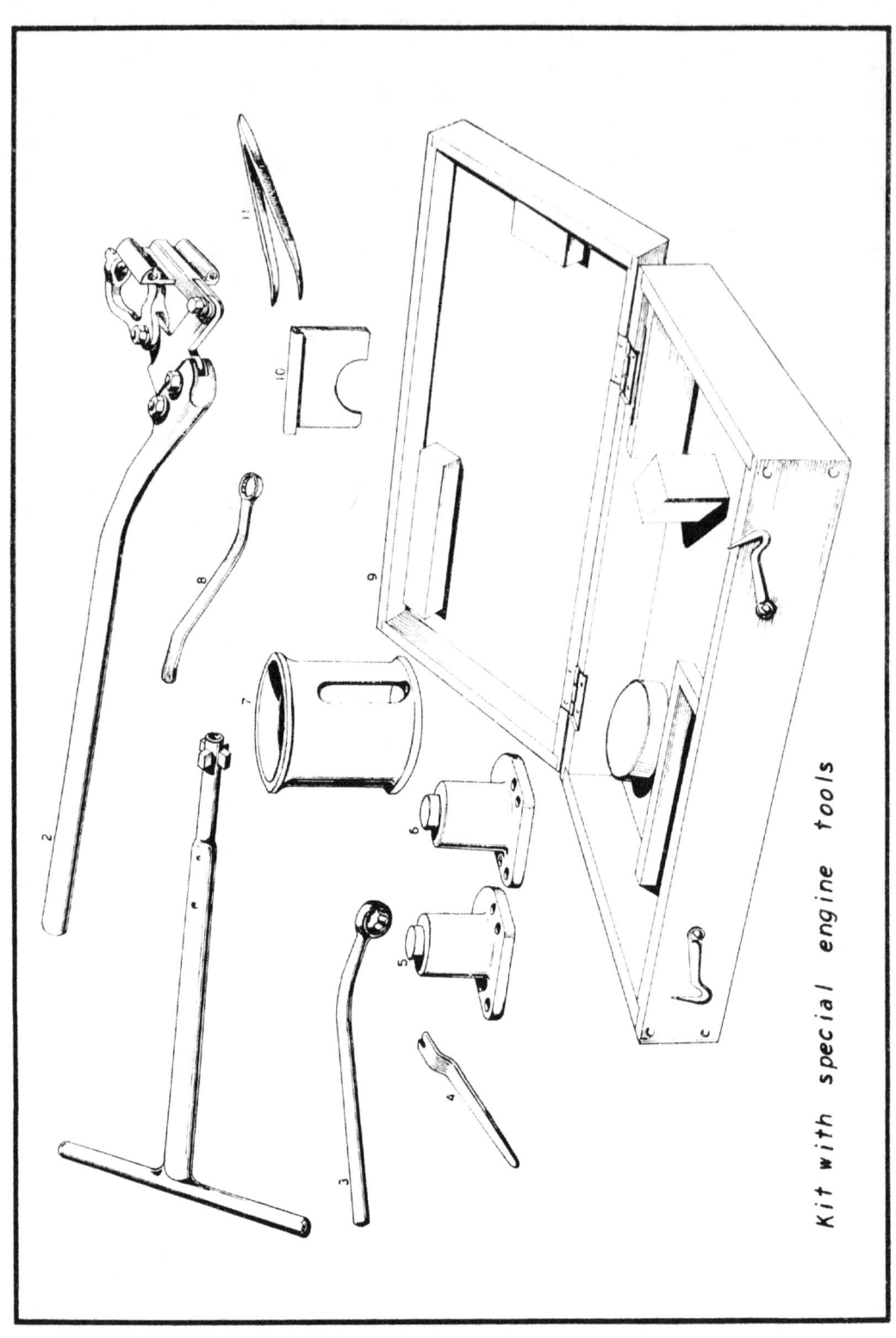

Kit with special engine tools

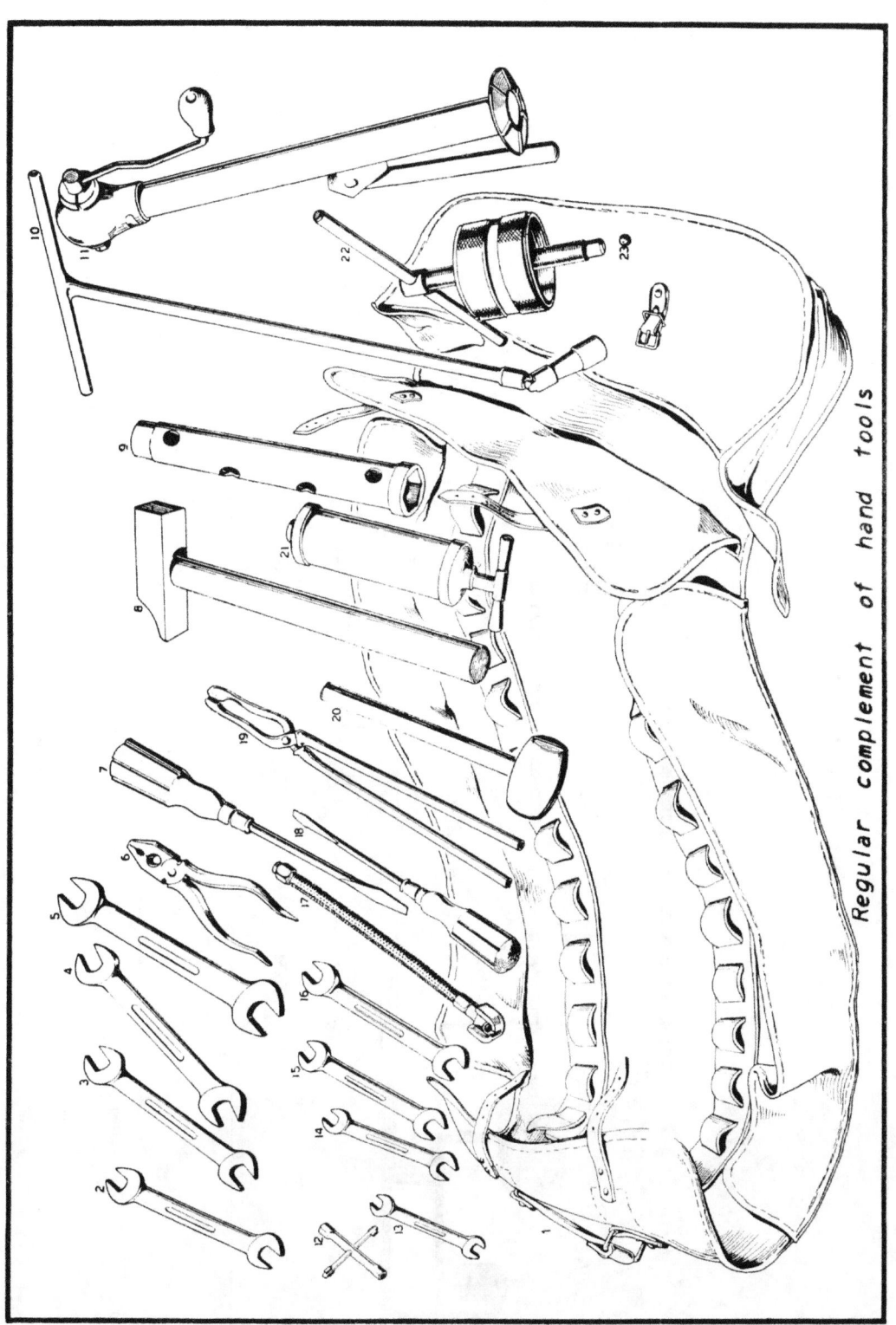

Regular complement of hand tools

ENGINE LUBRICATION

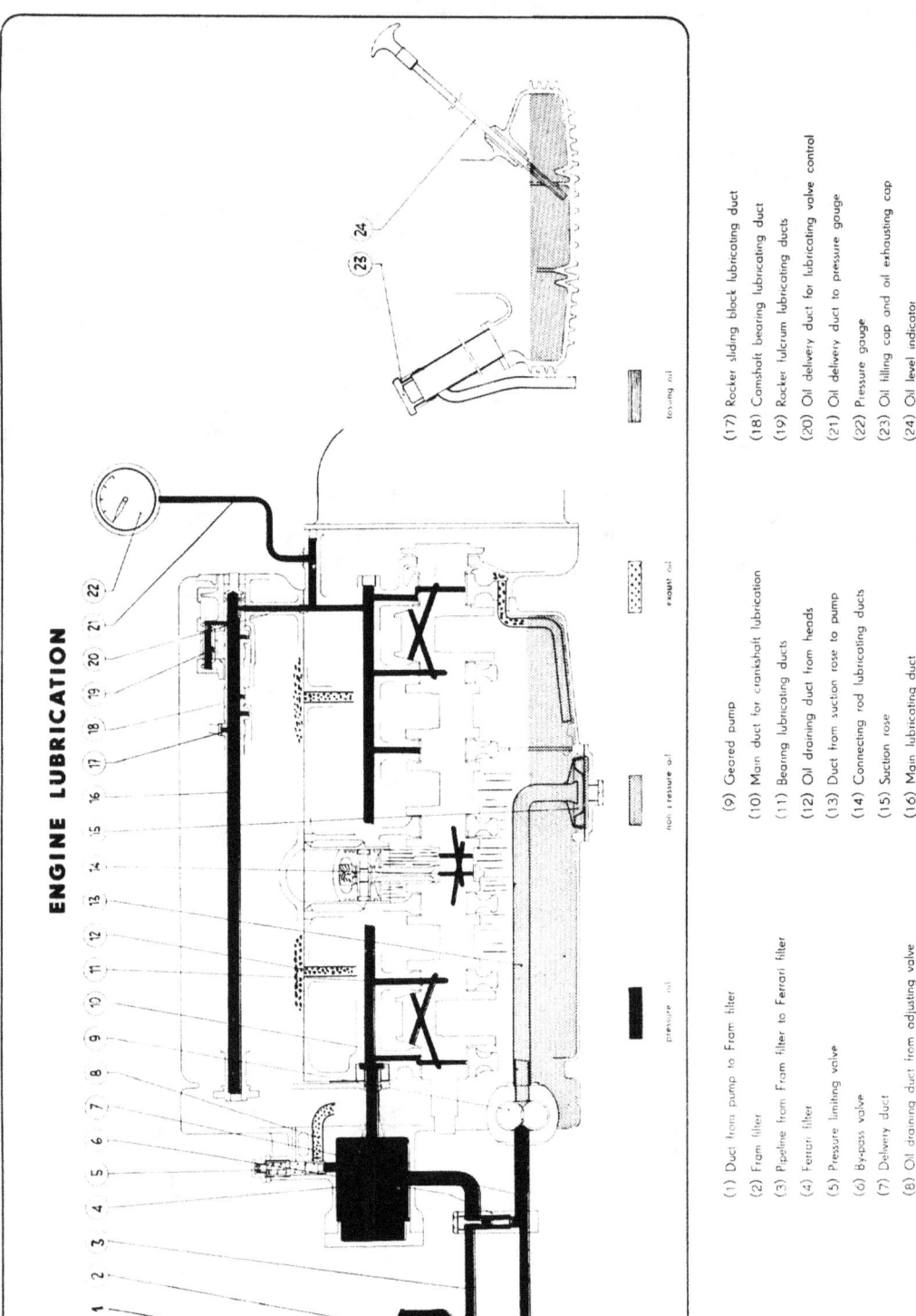

(1) Duct from pump to Fram filter
(2) Fram filter
(3) Pipeline from Fram filter to Ferrari filter
(4) Ferrari filter
(5) Pressure limiting valve
(6) By-pass valve
(7) Delivery duct
(8) Oil draining duct from adjusting valve
(9) Geared pump
(10) Main duct for crankshaft lubrication
(11) Bearing lubricating ducts
(12) Oil draining duct from heads
(13) Duct from suction rose to pump
(14) Connecting rod lubricating ducts
(15) Suction rose
(16) Main lubricating duct
(17) Rocker sliding block lubricating duct
(18) Camshaft bearing lubricating duct
(19) Rocker fulcrum lubricating ducts
(20) Oil delivery duct for lubricating valve control
(21) Oil delivery duct to pressure gauge
(22) Pressure gauge
(23) Oil filling cap and oil exhausting cap
(24) Oil level indicator

ENGINE LUBRICATION SYSTEM.

(1) Oil radiator.
(2) Tube from oil radiator to filter.
(3) Tube from oil radiator to thermostat.
(4) Filter.
(5) Oil pressure relief valve.
(6) Oil thermostat regulator.
(7) Pipe from pump to filter.
(8) Return oil pipe from relief valve.
(9) Oil pump.
(10) Main bearing oil gallery pipe.
(11) Oil passage to main bearings.
(12) Used oil return pipe.
(13) Inlet pipe to pump from sump.
(14) Big end lubrication arrangement.
(15) Filter entry to suction pipe.
(16) Oil gallery pipe for valve arrangement.
(17) Oil supply to valve tappets.
(18) Oil supply to cams.
(19) Oil supply to valve reelers.
(20) Supply to valves, gear oil gallery.
(21) Supply to oil gauge.
(22) Oil gauge.
(23) Oil filter.
(24) Dip stick.

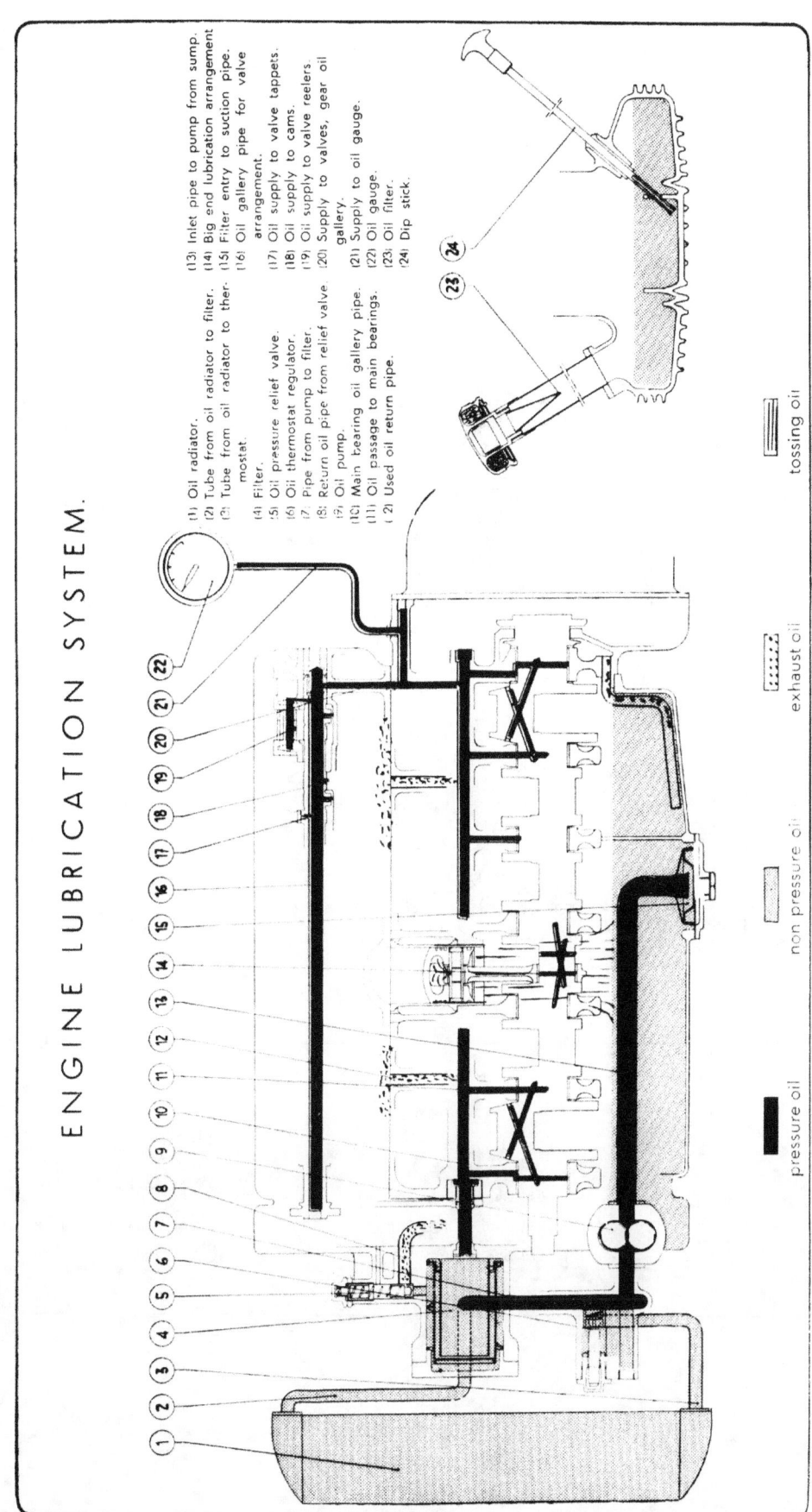

pressure oil — non pressure oil — exhaust oil — tossing oil

151

GENERAL LUBRICATION

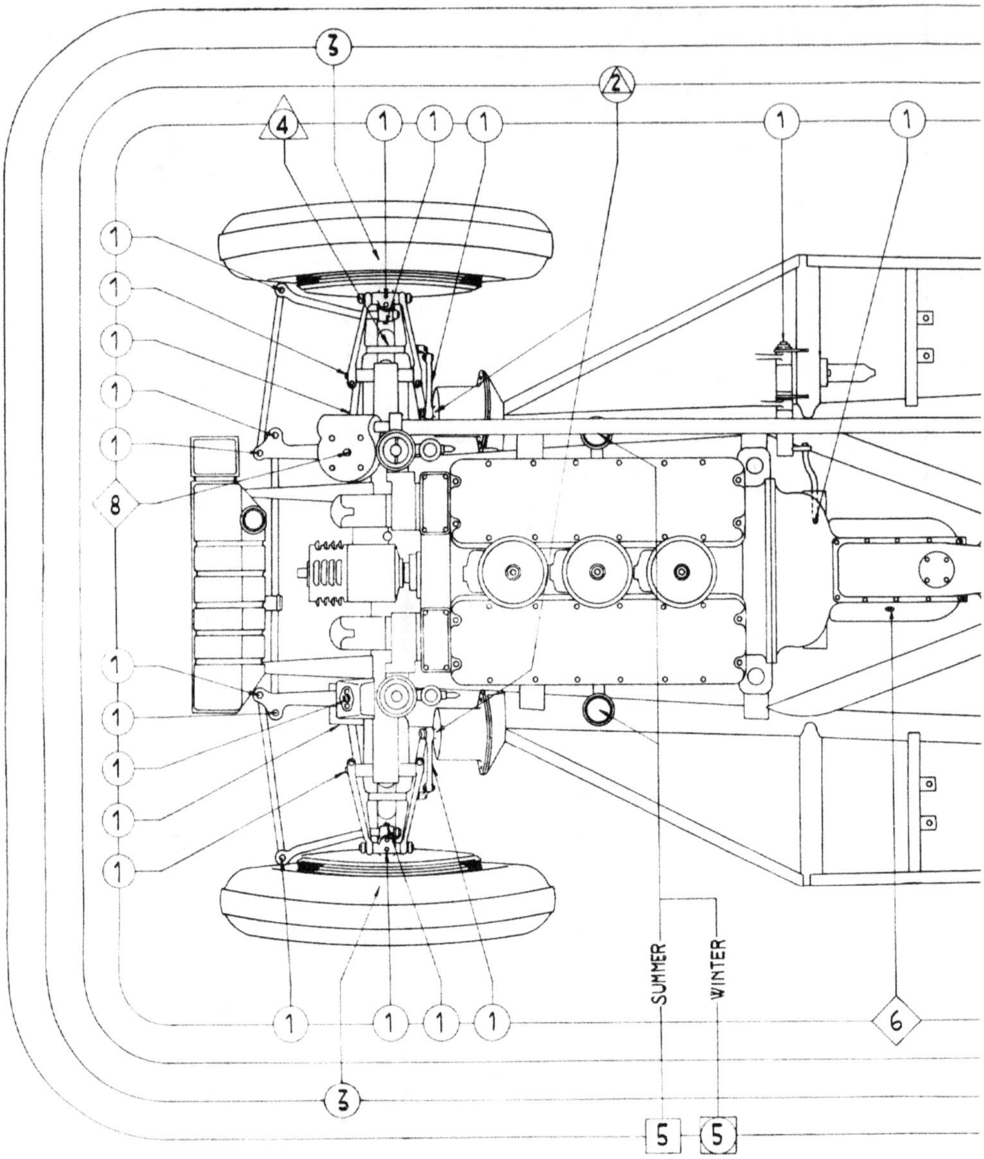

◇ Oil Shell x 100 SAE 40
⬭ Oil Shell x 100 SAE 30
☐ Oil Shell Spirax 90 EP

△ CASTOR OIL
△ Oil Shell Donax P
○ Grease

AND GREASING OF CHASSIS

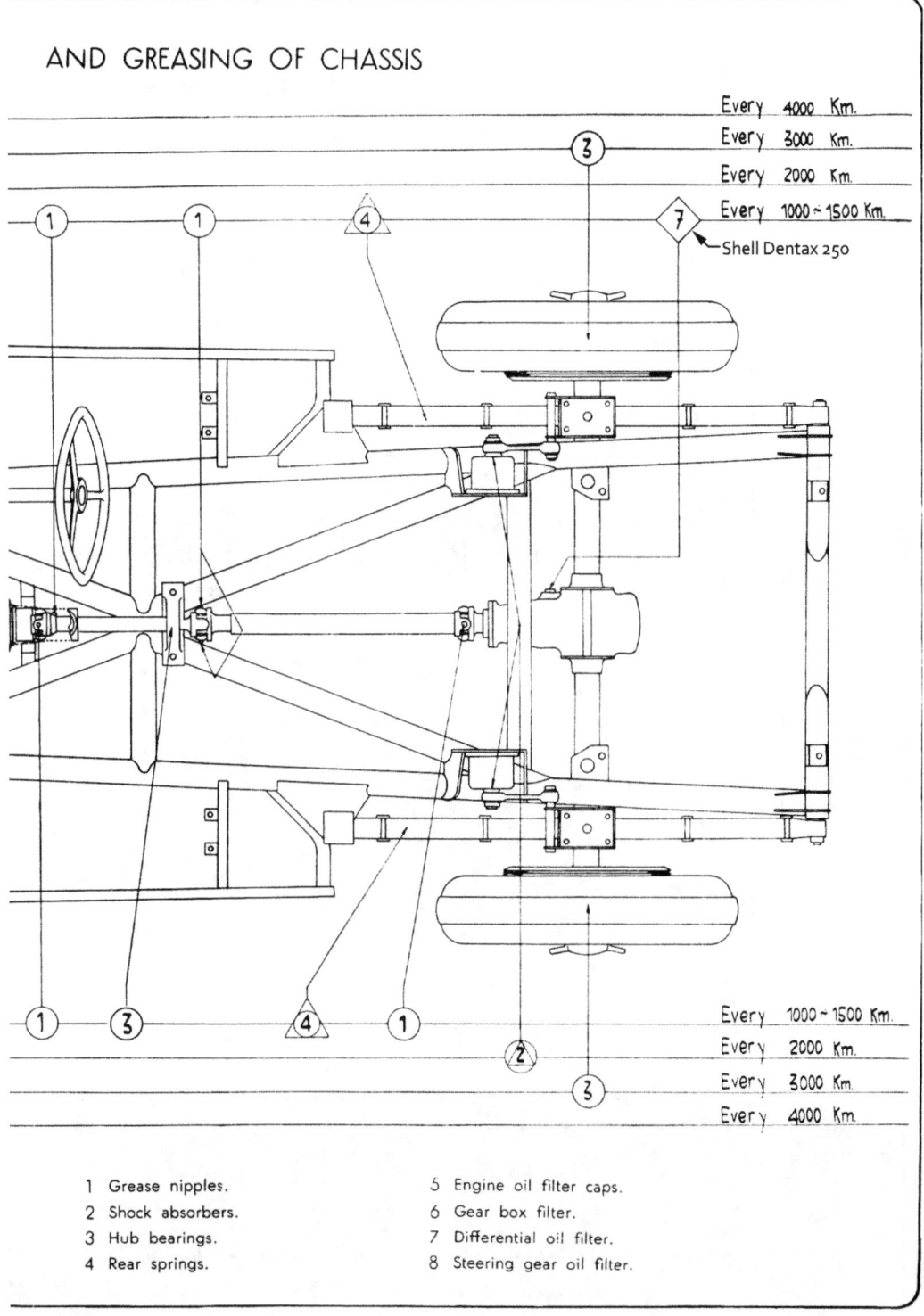

1 Grease nipples.
2 Shock absorbers.
3 Hub bearings.
4 Rear springs.
5 Engine oil filter caps.
6 Gear box filter.
7 Differential oil filter.
8 Steering gear oil filter.

GENERAL DIAGRAM OF

Capacity for lubricant of:

ENGINE TANK: 16 litres

REAR AXLE - GEARBOX: 3.5 litres

Never exceed maximum level
Never go below minimum level

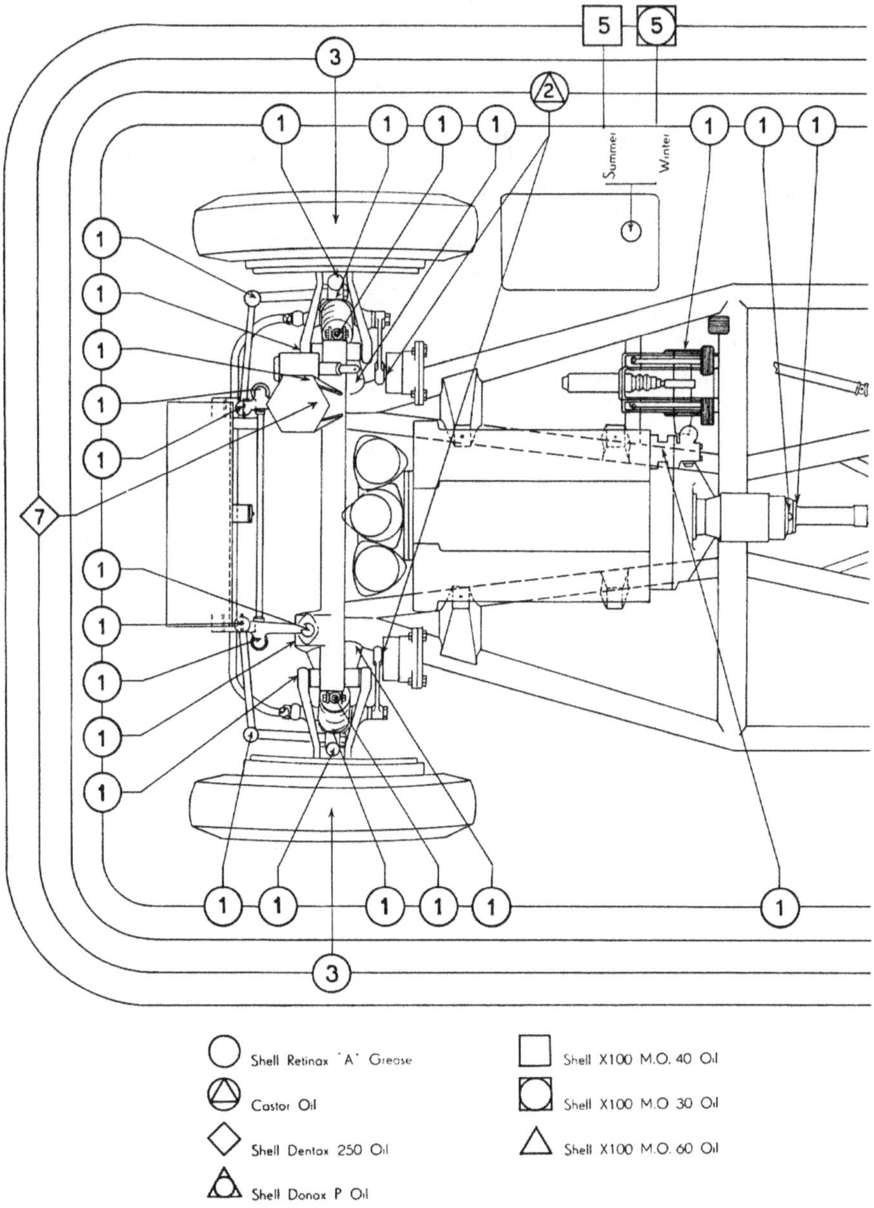

Summer | Winter

○ Shell Retinax 'A' Grease
◐ Castor Oil
◇ Shell Dentax 250 Oil
△ Shell Donax P Oil

□ Shell X100 M.O. 40 Oil
▢ Shell X100 M.O. 30 Oil
△ Shell X100 M.O. 60 Oil

LUBRICATION

N. B. - Before injecting the prescribed oil, by means of a grease gun, between the spring leaves, lift the car by means of a jack, take off the small bolts of the spring clips, and wash with petroleum.

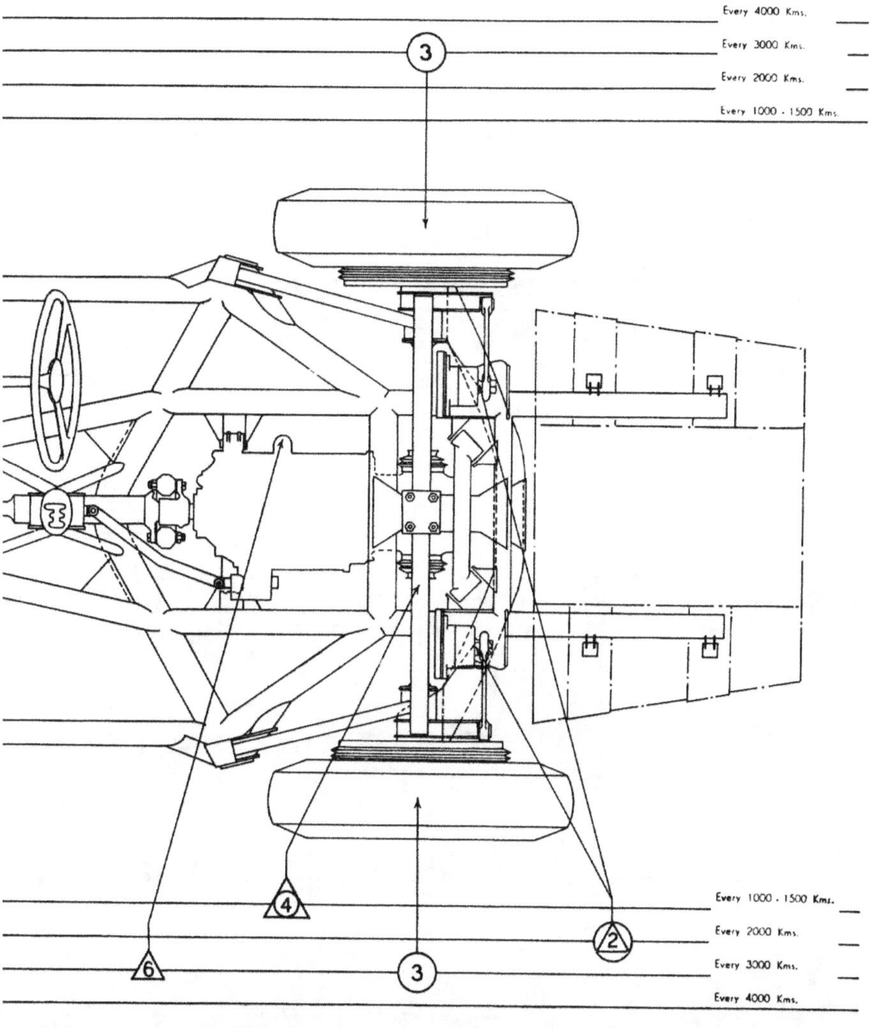

Every 4000 Kms.
Every 3000 Kms.
Every 2000 Kms.
Every 1000 - 1500 Kms.

Every 1000 - 1500 Kms.
Every 2000 Kms.
Every 3000 Kms.
Every 4000 Kms.

1 Oilers (Grease Nipplers)
2 Shock Absorbers
3 Bearings
4 Leaf Spring
5 Engine
6 Rear Axle - Gearbox
7 Steering Box

GENERAL LUBRICATION AND

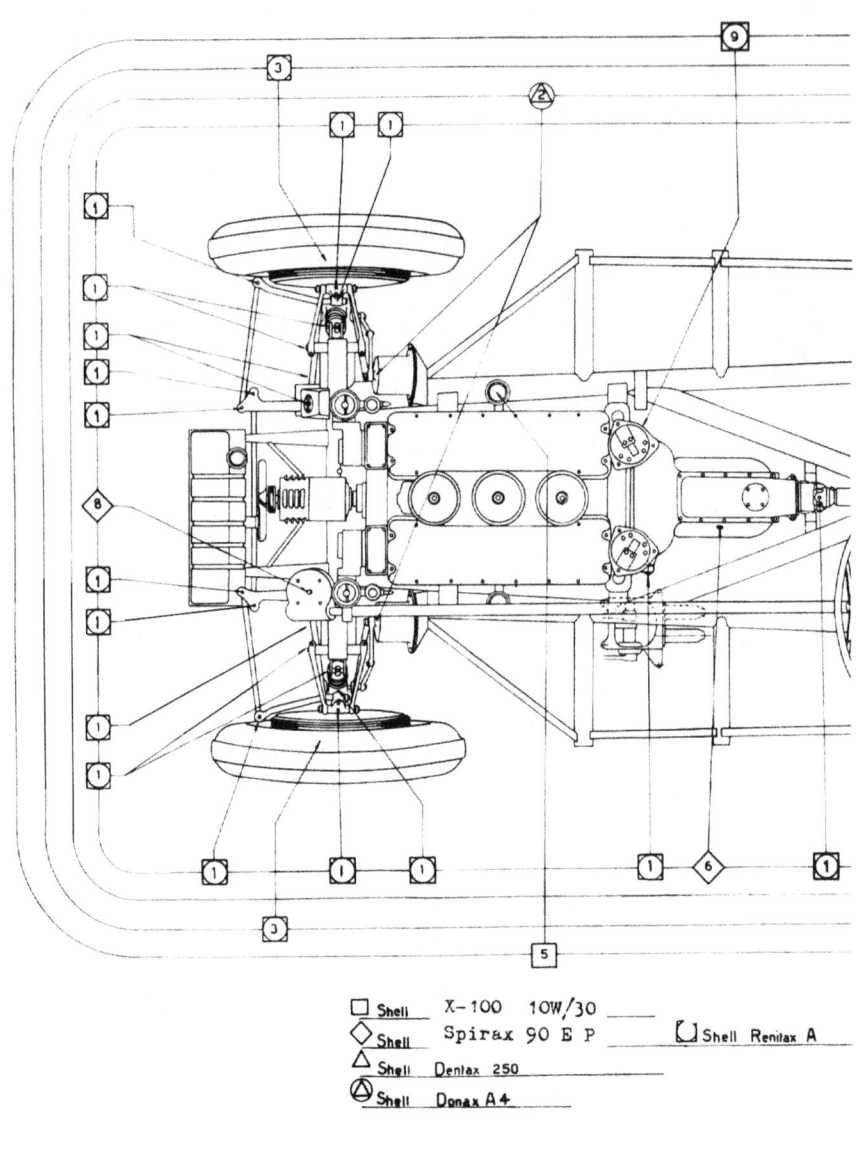

☐ Shell X-100 10W/30
◇ Shell Spirax 90 E P   ⌒ Shell Renitax A
△ Shell Dentax 250
⬬ Shell Donax A 4

GREASING OF CHASSIS

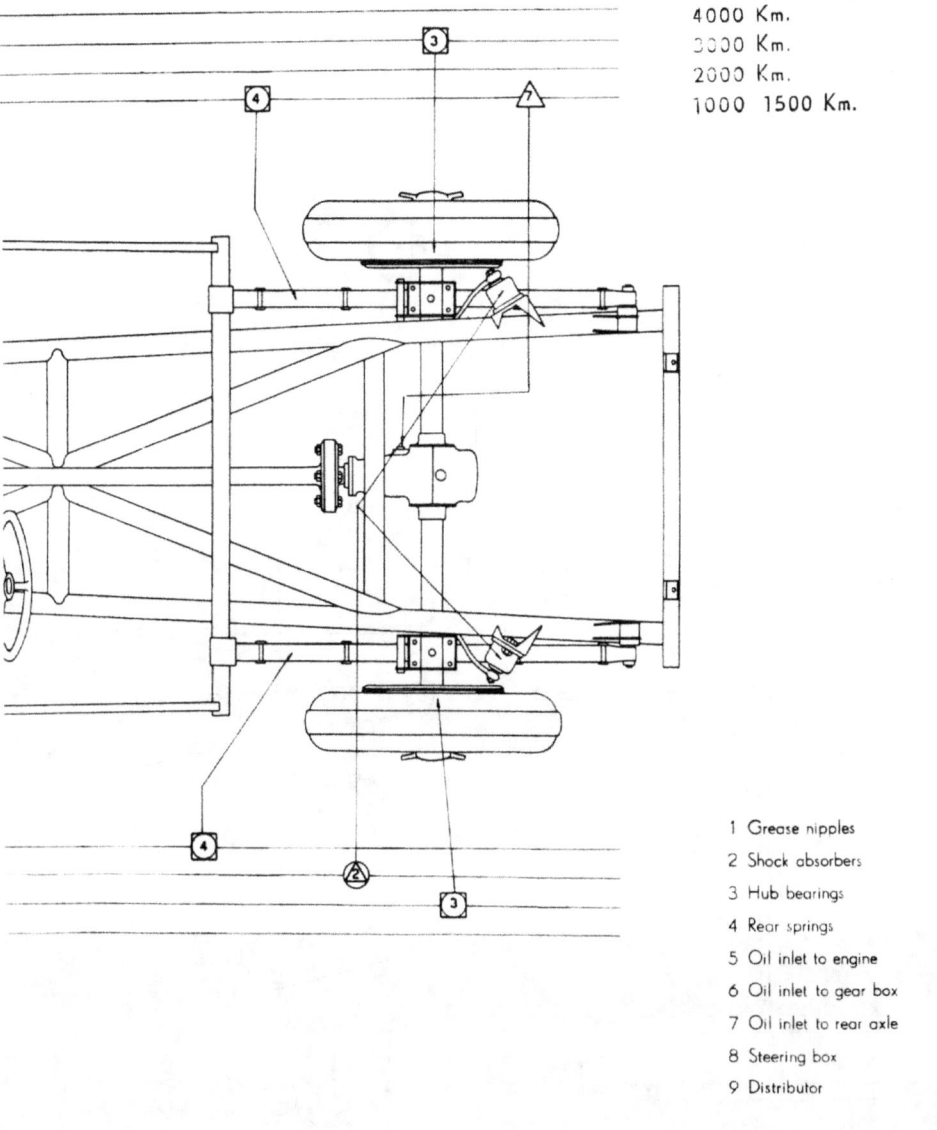

4000 Km.
3000 Km.
2000 Km.
1000 1500 Km.

1 Grease nipples
2 Shock absorbers
3 Hub bearings
4 Rear springs
5 Oil inlet to engine
6 Oil inlet to gear box
7 Oil inlet to rear axle
8 Steering box
9 Distributor

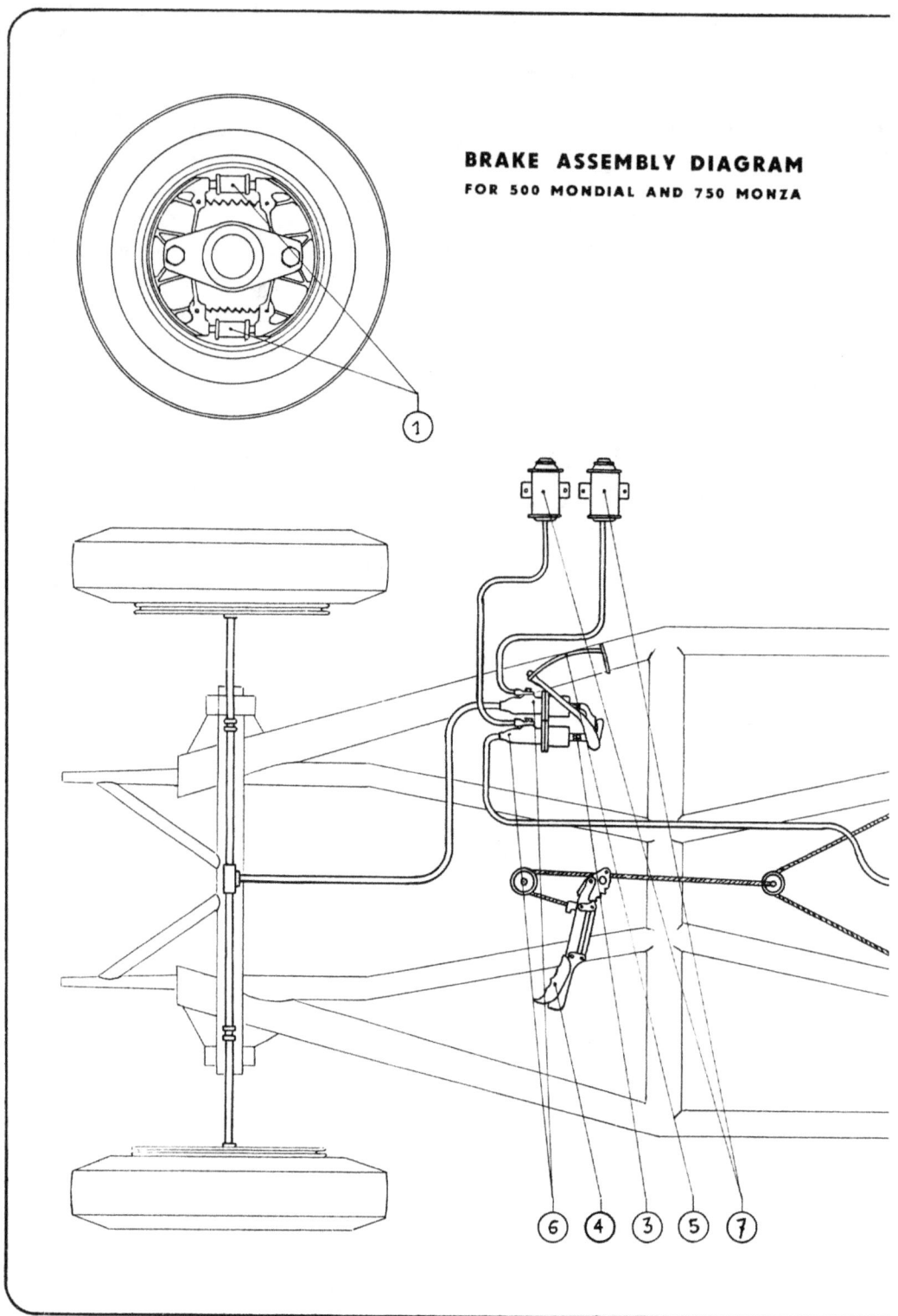

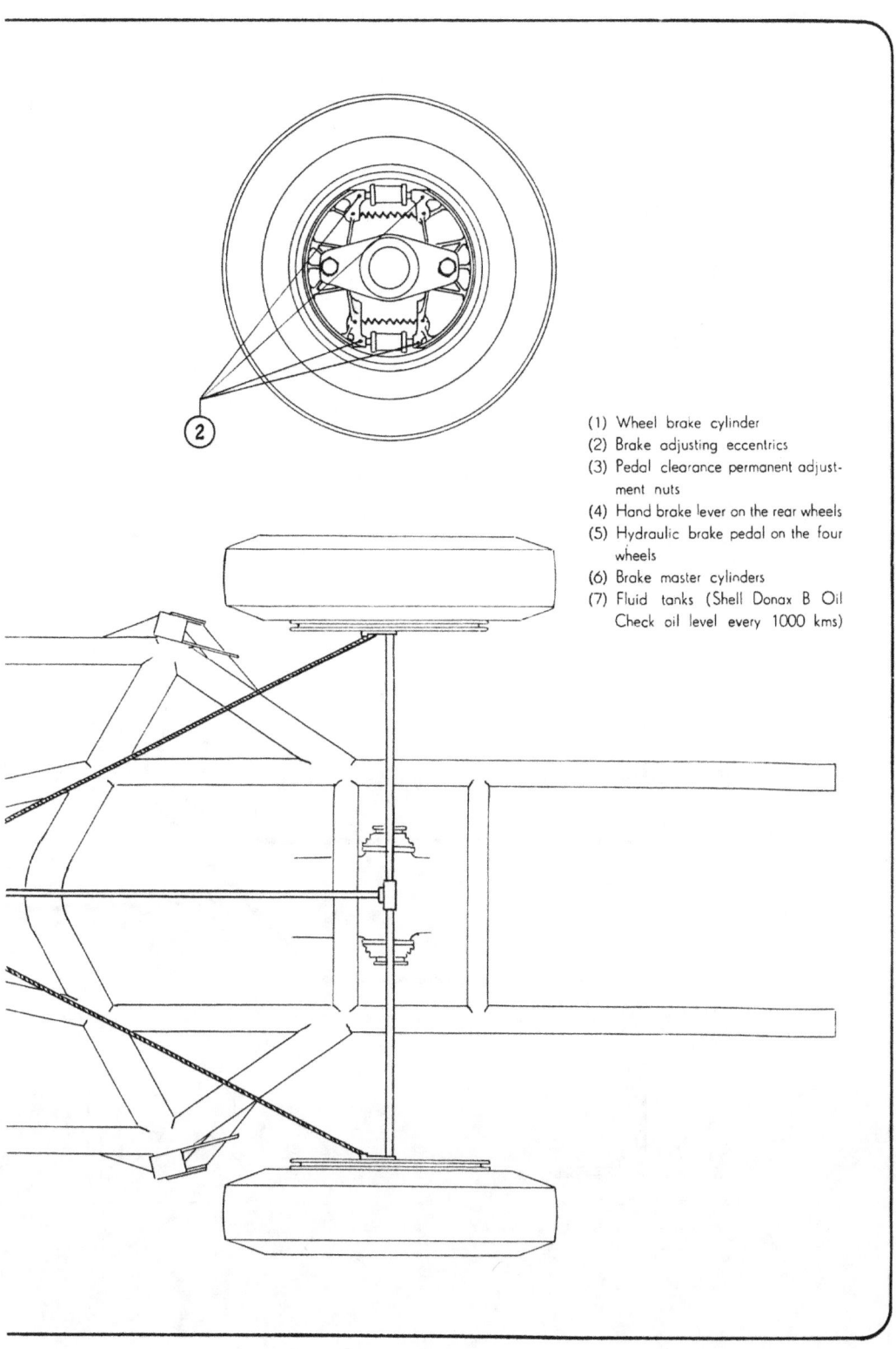

(1) Wheel brake cylinder
(2) Brake adjusting eccentrics
(3) Pedal clearance permanent adjustment nuts
(4) Hand brake lever on the rear wheels
(5) Hydraulic brake pedal on the four wheels
(6) Brake master cylinders
(7) Fluid tanks (Shell Donax B Oil Check oil level every 1000 kms)

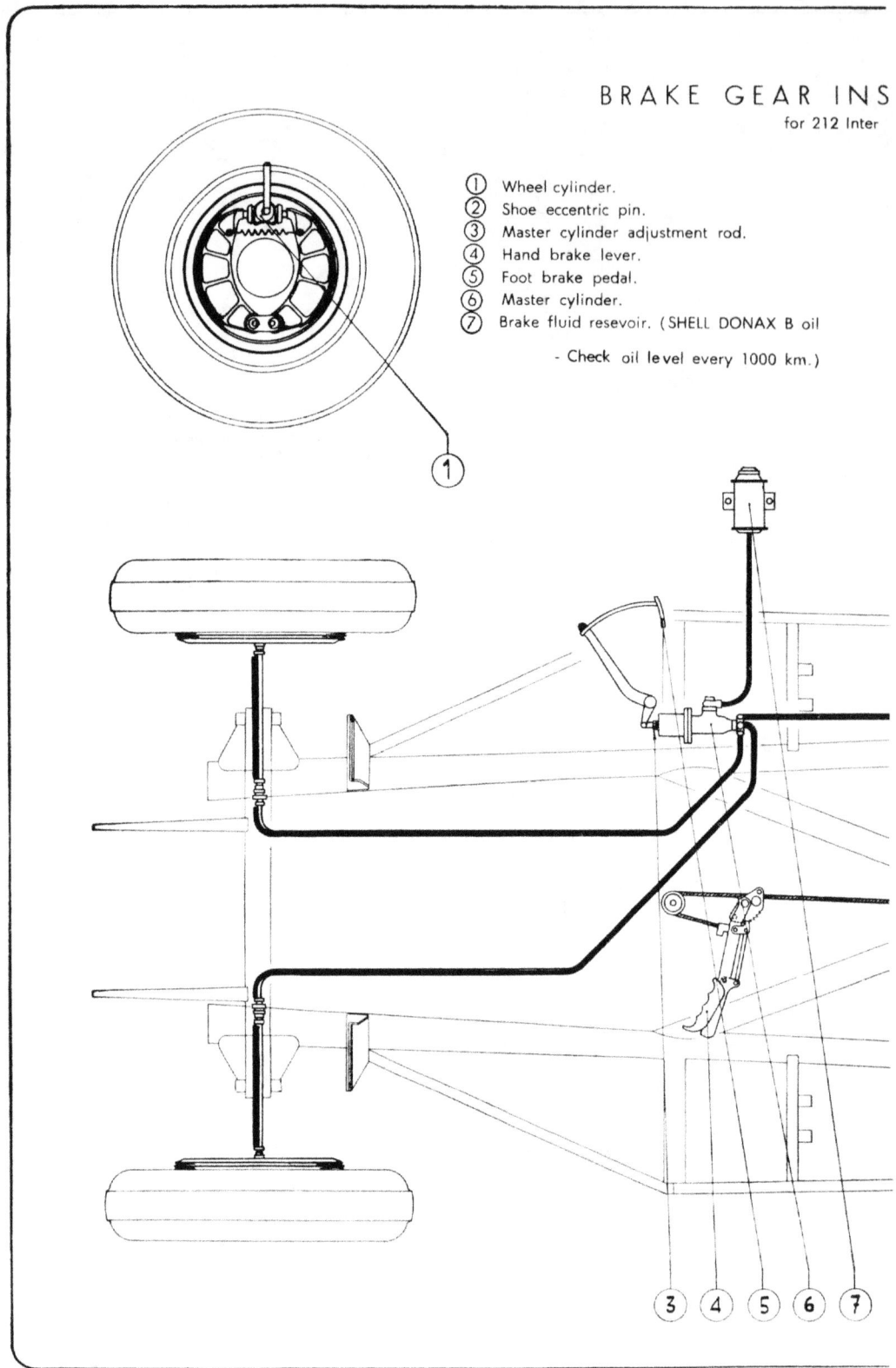

BRAKE GEAR INS
for 212 Inter

1. Wheel cylinder.
2. Shoe eccentric pin.
3. Master cylinder adjustment rod.
4. Hand brake lever.
5. Foot brake pedal.
6. Master cylinder.
7. Brake fluid resevoir. (SHELL DONAX B oil
   - Check oil level every 1000 km.)

TRUCTIONS

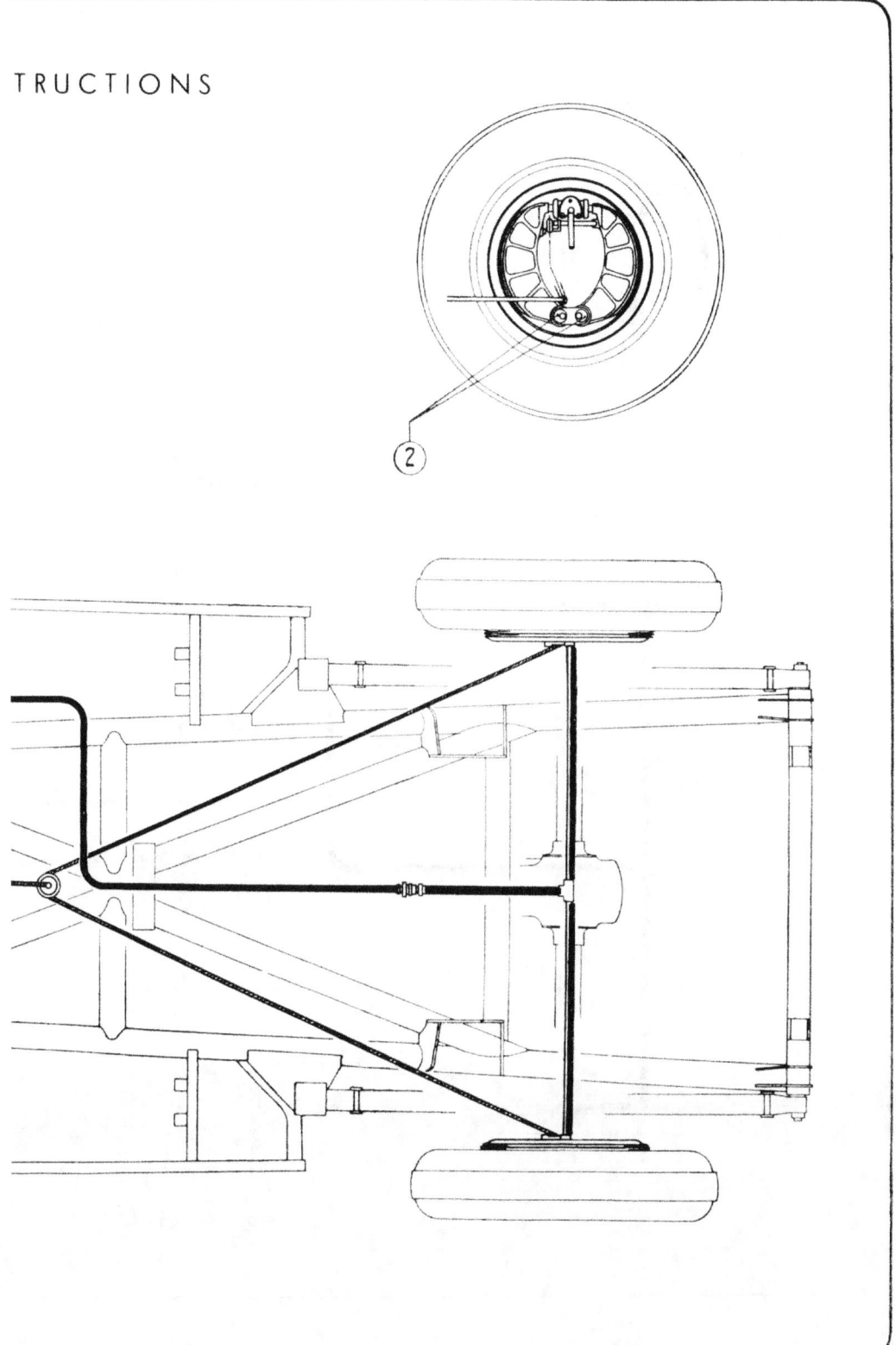

BRAKE GEAR INST

for 250 MILLEMIGLIA - 340 MILLEMIGLIA

1. Wheel cylinder.
2. Shoe eccentric pin.
3. Master cylinder adjustment rod.
4. Hand brake lever.
5. Foot brake pedal.
6. Master cylinder.
7. Brake fluid resevoir. (SHELL DONAX B oil
     - Check oil level every 1000 km.)

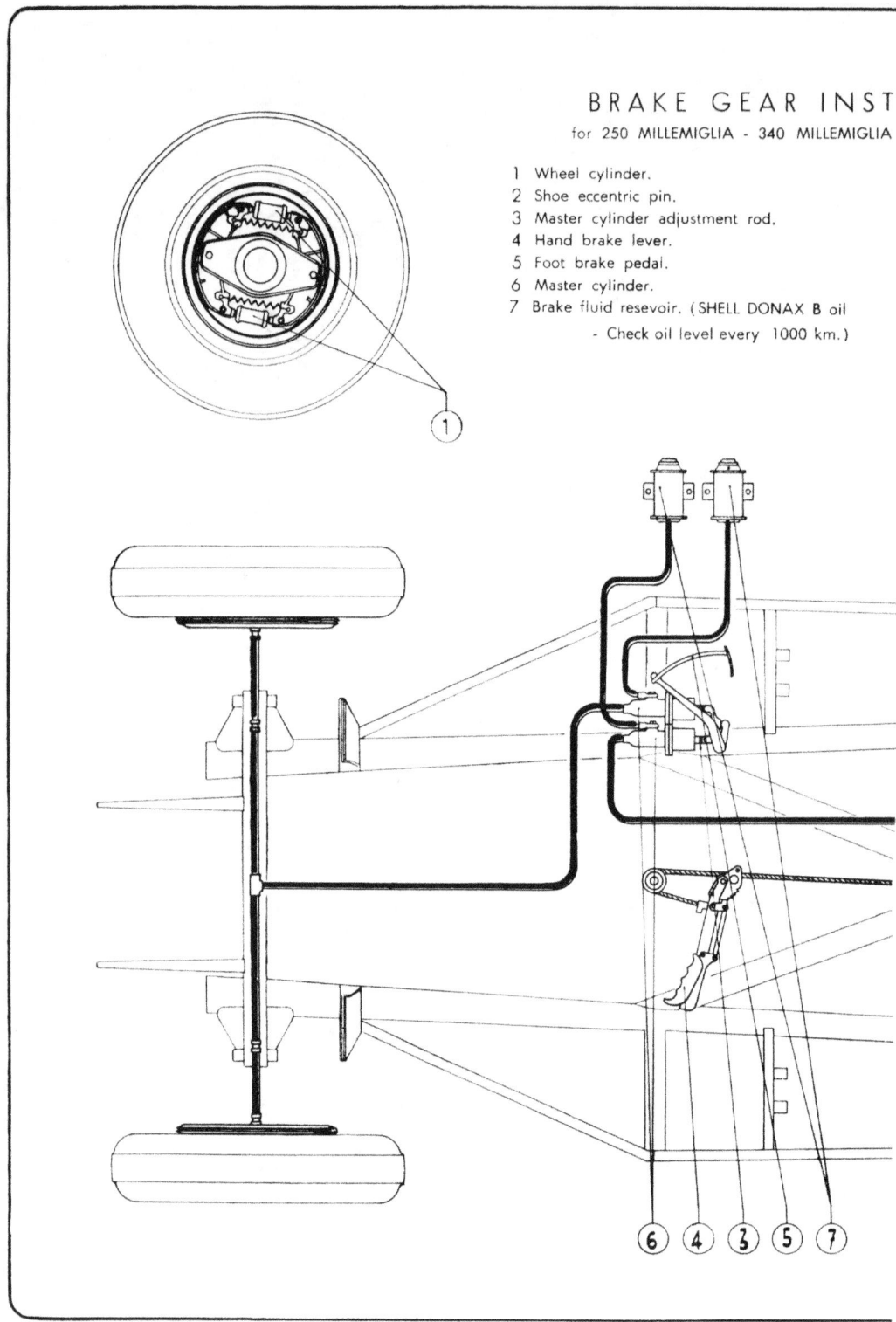

RUCTIONS
- 342 AMERICA CARS

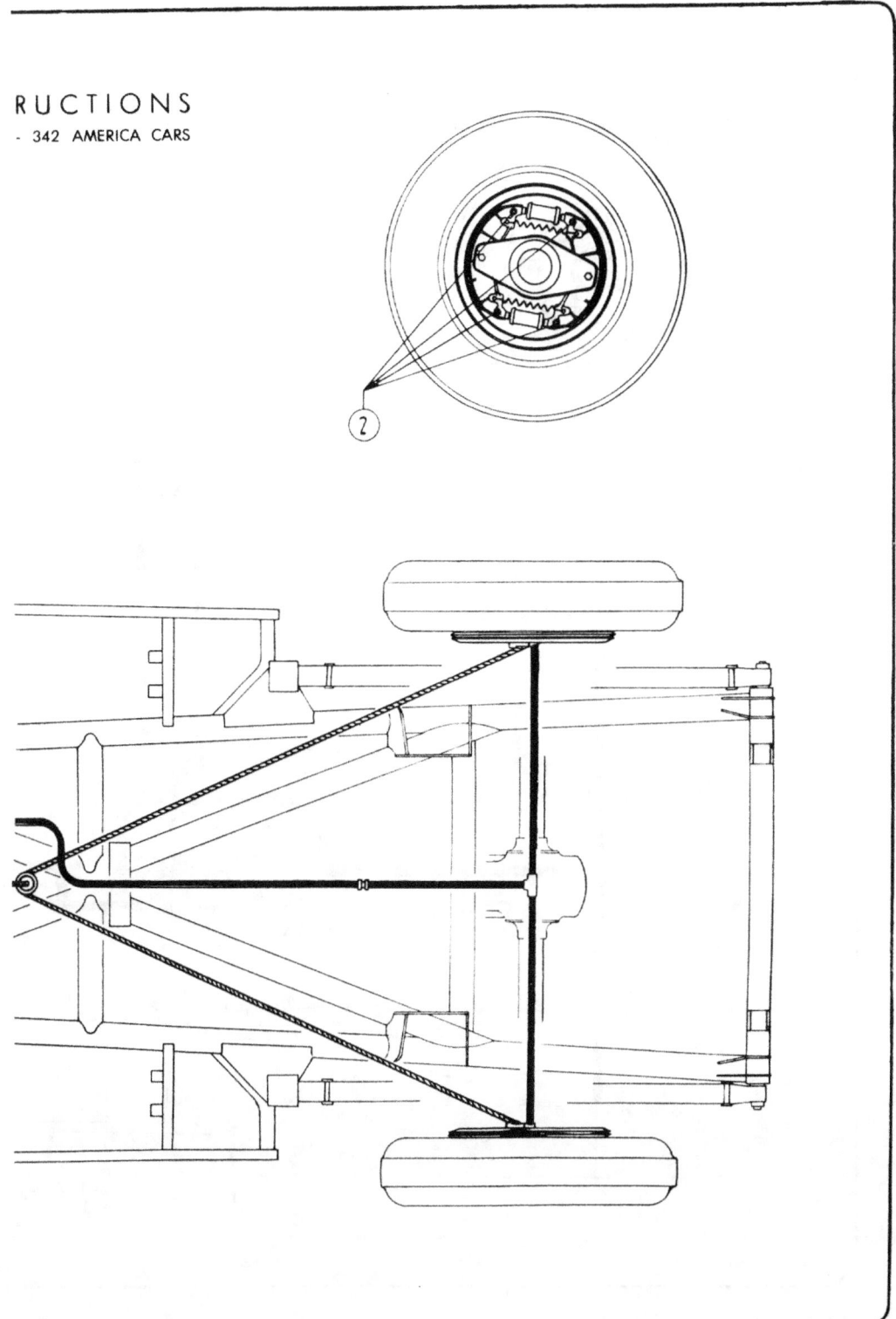

BRAKE

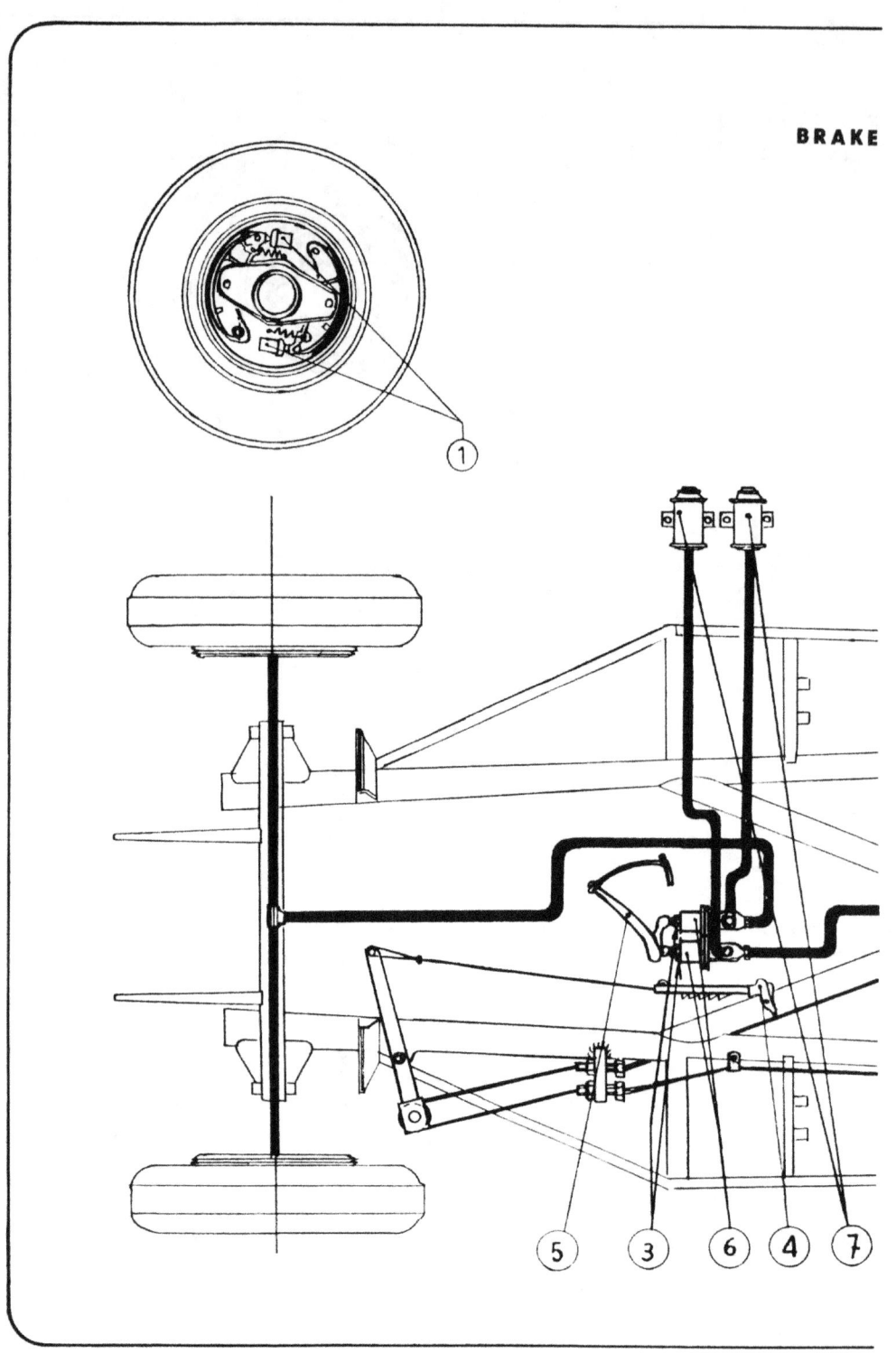

ASSEMBLY

1) Wheel brake cylinders
2) Adjusting cams
3) Brake adjuster
4) Hand brake lever on rear wheels
5) Brake pedal on four wheels
6) Brake master cylinders
7) Oil tanks (SHELL DONAX B oil - check oil level every 1000 kms)

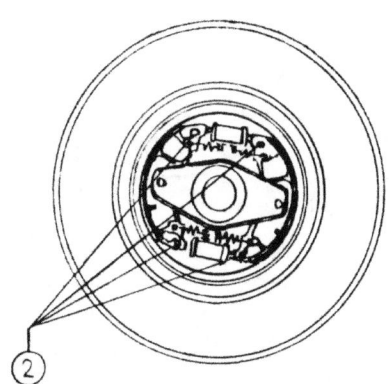

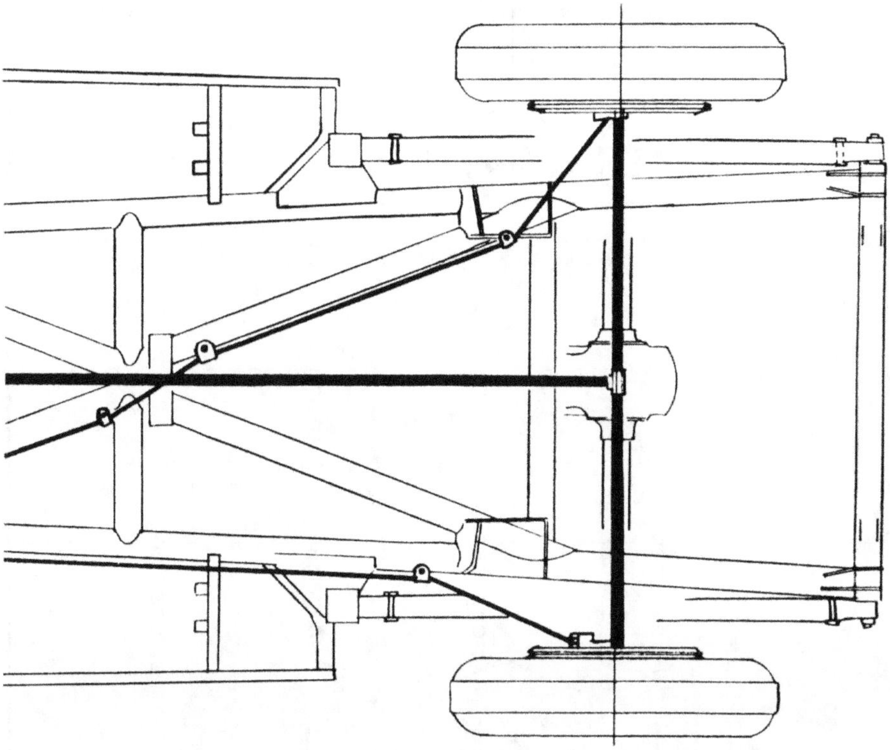

DIAGRAM OF RING INSTALLATION ON THE PISTONS
FOR 500 MONDIAL AND 750 MONZA CARS

A — Arrangement of tapering in A

B — Arrangement of tapering in B

C — Arrangement of tapering in C

D — Scraper ring in D

Jackie Ginther at the wheel of one of the latest Ferrari models, the "California".

Mechanical specifications of the "California" are those of the 250 Gran Turismo: 2953 cc. V-12 (180 cu. ins.) of 260 horsepower. It will do the standing quarter mile in 15.6 seconds.

ferrari 250 granturismo coupé pininfarina 2+2

engine

Number and arrangement of cylinders	V - 12 - 60°
Bore and stroke	73 x 58.8 mm
Piston displacement	2953,211 cc.
Compression ratio	8,8 : 1
Maximum b.h.p. at 7000 r.p.m.	240

Crankshaft on 7 bearings and connecting rods coupled in parallel on thin wall bearings
Cylinder block and silumin crankcase with forced-in liners
V-overhead valves with screw adjustable cams and roller rockers
Camshafts and water pump driven by a silent chain with turn-buckle tightener
Lubrication by geared pump
Battery ignition and two distributors with automatic timing advance
Feeding by one diaphragm fuel pump and one self-regulating electric pump
Carburization by three double-bodied carburettors
Dry clutch and elastic hub
Cooling by multitubular water radiator and automatic fan, patent Peugeot.

chassis

Gear box with 4 silent synchromesh speeds, operated by a central lever, direct drive on the 4th speed, 5th automatic « overdrive »
Rear axle of the stiff type with lateral rods
Rear suspension with semi-elliptic leaf-springs, and large telescopic shockabsorbers
Front suspension with independent wheels, and helicoidal springs, telescopic shockabsorbers
Single-block steel tubular frame
Steering unit with independent links. Left hand drive
Disc-brakes on the four wheels, mechanic hand control on the rear wheels

Wheelbase 2600 mm	front tread 1354 mm
	rear tread 1394 mm
Weight of the empty car: 1280 kgs.	
Fuel tank capacity: 100 l.	

Fuel consumption every 100 kms, approx. 16 l.
Light alloy wire wheels for tires size 650 x 15 or 185 x 15

speeds attainable a 7000 r.p.m.

back axle ratio	1st speed	2nd speed	3rd speed	4th speed	In 4th speed x 1000 revs
7/32	54 mph	76 mph	102 mph	126 mph	18 mph
8/34	58 mph	82 mph	110 mph	135 mph	20 mph
8/32	61 mph	85 mph	115 mph	144 mph	21 mph

The 5th automatic « overdrive » increases of 22% the speed of the direct drive in 4th gear and is fitted with the 7/32 ratio only

These data are for information only

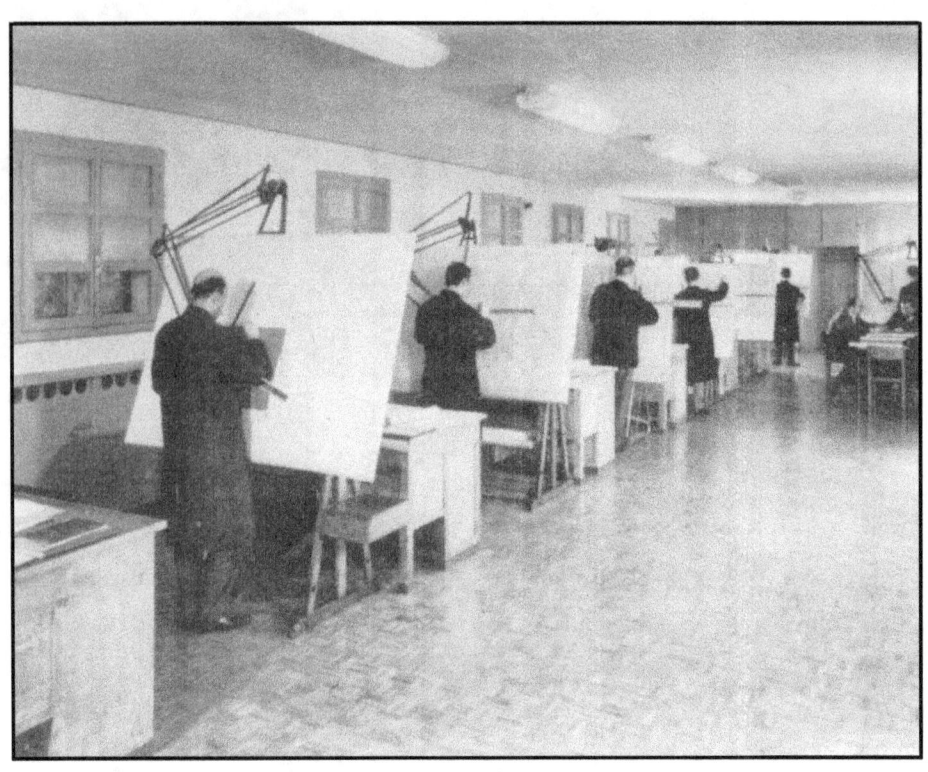
Design and development is a big factor at Ferrari.

Ferrari maintains its own foundry for casting light metal.

Ferrari's modern shop is equipped with the latest in precision machinery.

Engine block casting is machined under close inspection.

Final assembly of Ferrari engines is carried out in a separate small room off the main shop.

Racing department makes use of dynamometers in spotless test room.

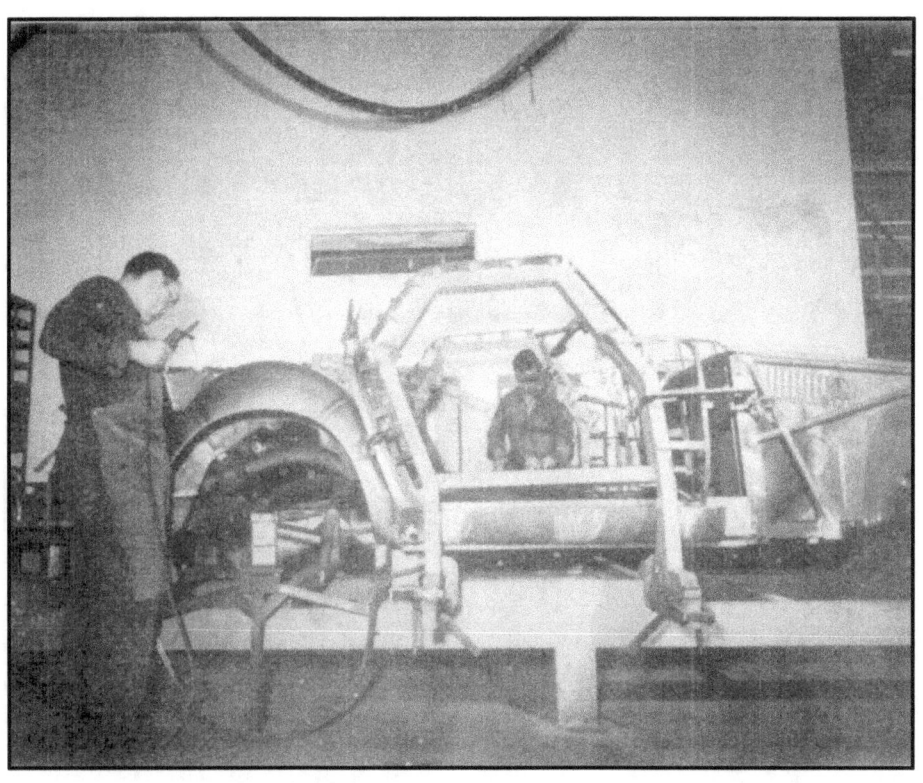

Pinin Farina bodies for Ferrari begin on welding jigs.

Berlinetta coupe takes shape on body jig.

Completed cars pass bare frames as they leave factory.

Farina bodies on moving line receive finishing touches.

www.ingramcontent.com/pod-product-compliance
Lightning Source LLC
Chambersburg PA
CBHW082204230426
43672CB00015B/2892